# TEN DAYS TO PEACE

# TEN DAYS TO PEACE

*A ten day guided journey to find peace through God's grace.*

## Britton Mikael George

**BRITTON**
*Mikael George*

Published by Written by Britton

Copyright © 2025 by Britton Mikael George

All rights reserved.

No portion of this book may be reproduced in any form without written permission from the publisher or author, except as permitted by U.S. copyright law.

This publication is designed to provide accurate and authoritative information in regard to the subject matter covered. It is sold with the understanding that neither the author nor the publisher is engaged in rendering legal, investment, accounting or other professional services. While the publisher and author have used their best efforts in preparing this book, they make no representations or warranties with respect to the accuracy or completeness of the contents of this book and specifically disclaim any implied warranties of merchantability or fitness for a particular purpose. No warranty may be created or extended by sales representatives or written sales materials. The advice and strategies contained herein may not be suitable for your situation. You should consult with a professional when appropriate. Neither the publisher nor the author shall be liable for any loss of profit or any other commercial damages, including but not limited to special, incidental, consequential, personal, or other damages.

All Scripture quotations, unless otherwise indicated, are taken from the Holy Bible, New International Version®, NIV®. Copyright ©1973, 1978, 1984, 2011 by Biblica, Inc.™ Used by permission of Zondervan. All rights reserved worldwide. www.zondervan.comThe "NIV" and "New International Version" are trademarks registered in the United States Patent and Trademark Office by Biblica, Inc.™

Scripture quotations marked CSB have been taken from the Christian Standard Bible®, Copyright © 2017 by Holman Bible Publishers. Used by permission. Christian Standard Bible® and CSB® are federally registered trademarks of Holman Bible Publishers.

Scripture taken from the New King James Version®. Copyright © 1982 by Thomas Nelson. Used by permission. All rights reserved.

Book Cover by Britton Mikael George. © All rights reserved.
1st edition 2024

*All the glory to God.*
*All my love to my husband and children.*

*To anyone feeling beat down by the world, this one's for you.*

Gifted to:
_____

From:
_____

Date:
_____

# Contents

Playlist .................................................... ix
Preface ..................................................... x

## Day One
Defining Your "It" and Creating Room for God's Best ................. 1

## Day Two
Mindset: Surrendering My Self-Criticism ........................ 16

## Day Three
Identity: Surrending My False Self-Image ........................ 26

## Day Four
Moving Out of Fear and Into Favor ............................. 34

## Day Five
Looking Beyond Discomfort and Inconvenience .................. 43

## Day Six
Cultivating My Soil ........................................... 52

## Day Seven
Grace for Self: Seeking Personal Peace .......................... 62

## Day Eight
Forgiveness of Others: Seeking Relational Peace .................. 72

## Day Nine
Seeking Spiritual Peace ....................................... 83

## Day Ten
Peace I Leave With You ....................................... 89

Acknowledgements ........................................... 95
About the Author ............................................ 97

# *Playlist*

**Make Room**
The Church Will Sing

**You Say**
Lauren Daigle

**Who You Say I Am**
Hillsong Worship

**Good Plans**
Red Rocks Worship ft. Cody Carnes

**Hard Fought Hallelujah**
Brandon Lake

**Honey in the Rock**
Brooke Ligertwood & Brandon Lake

**God Really Loves Us**
Crowder, Dante Bowe, & Maverick City Music

**Chain Breaker**
Zach Williams

**Same God**
Elevation Worship ft. Jonsal Barrientes

**The Blessing (Live)**
Elevation Worship, Kari Jobe, & Cody Carnes

# Preface

Give it to God

We hear it suggested, preached, and repeated over and over. Yet, while Giving it to God is a powerful and important concept, it's not so easy. How do I give it to God, exactly? Do I physically hand it off? Throw it at Him while yelling some not-so-nice words I would need to repent for later? Will God just come down and take it from me (pretty please)? Do I just pray about it until it goes away? Give it to God is more than a pretty sentiment. In fact, it's biblical—but, how exactly do I do it?

God commands us to "fear not" more than any other command in the Bible. He tells us, "Do not be afraid," "Be strong and courageous," "Do not be discouraged," and "Do not be anxious" exactly 365 times. Our God is not coincidental. Every single day, we face fears, anxieties, and frustrations that steal our peace. Failing relationships, financial strain, health crises, a never-ending to-do list, familial responsibilities, and on and on, it goes. Every single day, we need a reminder not to fear, but to give our anxieties and fears to God, and that's exactly what God has given us—daily reminders of hope in those 365 passages. Isn't He amazing?

Fear comes from the enemy, while peace comes from resting in God and his promises. So, how do we focus less on the fears and move toward peace? My prayer for you as you work through these next ten days is that you will find the answer to this question and, ultimately, find true peace. My prayer is that the enemy would lose his grip on you and the Holy Spirit would work in you to keep that peace.

My prayer is that this devotional study will serve as a way to put actionable steps into place to take your "it" and give it to Him. And, my prayer is that, although not all of it will be pretty, you ultimately enjoy the process. But, I need to be real with you—you'll have to be real with yourself. You will have to acknowledge your pitfalls, your hurts, your self-criticism, doubt, and shame. The process can be painful, but I know from personal experience it is also cathartic. I cannot promise that every discomfort, anxiety, or hurt you feel will completely disappear in ten days, but I can promise you this book will serve as a powerful starting point where you can posture yourself toward healing and accepting God's never-ending and abundant grace. Get it, sis! ♥*Britt*

*"Fear not, for I am with you; Be not dismayed, for I am your God. I will strengthen you, Yes, I will help you, I will uphold you with My righteous right hand."*
*(Isaiah 41:10 NKJV)*

## How to use this book:

I've written this book in the hope that it serves as a tool for you. Each of the ten lessons will take between 30 and 60 minutes to complete and is broken into a daily scripture, worship song, reading, and journal prompt. So break out your colored pens, stickers, and sticky notes if you're into that or just grab the closest writing utensil within reach if that's your thing. Make this book your own! Use it to reflect, transform, and heal. Worship at the top of your lungs in your car to the daily music, or play it through your headphones as you meditate on the words during your lunch break. Make this book well used—crease, scribble, draw, highlight—it's not meant to be kept pretty. It's meant to be yours. ♥

## Scripture:

Each day a scripture will be given. Spend some time reflecting on God's Word. Pull open your Bible if you wish to dig into the entire chapter, or just focus on the passage provided. It's up to you— just give yourself the time you need. I know life is busy, but we are setting a big goal for a ten day period, so I would encourage you to be intentional in setting aside time just for yourself, so you can really dive in and spend time with God. ♥

## Playlist:

This book comes with a playlist! (How trendy am I?) But truly, is there anything more powerful than worshiping God through music to feel the presence of the Holy Spirit? The full playlist can be found by searching "Ten Days to Peace" on Spotify or just searching for each song on your preferred app. While I've listed the daily song at the beginning of each day, feel free to listen and worship at whichever point makes sense for you. Do you like to worship first to posture yourself for the upcoming message? Or do you prefer to worship after, in reflection? Or, maybe both! You do you, boo.♥

## Reading:

Each daily reading has a main theme. These themes relate to each step that we will work through: Surrender, Gratitude, Grace, Forgiveness, and Peace. The readings are meant to inspire and also give you actionable steps on your journey of healing, finding calm, or whatever particular sense of peace you are looking for. I will share some of my testimony in hopes of being vulnerable enough that it allows you to be vulnerable with yourself and God. I will encourage you to think critically and draw connections to your own weaknesses and battles, enabling you to find areas to loosen your grip—or let go completely—and find what you came here to find. You got this! ♥

## Journal:

Each reading passage will be followed by a journal prompt (and sometimes they're also sprinkled throughout the day's reading) so that you can just let it all out. Make this your safe space. Be honest with yourself and God. Putting fears and worries along with hopes and prayers into writing can be so cathartic. Anyone who has ever kept a diary or journal can tell you from experience—sometimes things make it to the paper before you even realize it was a thought. Write it all down! Word vomit your heart out. No shame here, friend!♥

## Prayer:

Finally, we will end each day with a prayer. While I will give you a prayer to read to yourself or aloud, I encourage you to continue the conversation with God beyond what is on the page. Give Him all of your praises, worries, hurts, thanks, and frustrations. He's got you.♥

## Actionable Steps Towards Peace

Surrender → Gratitude → Grace → Forgiveness → Peace

# Step 1

*Surrender*

# Day One

## Defining Your "It" and Creating Room for God's Best

 Playlist: Make Room

*"As for me, I will call upon God, And the Lord shall save me. Evening and morning and at noon I will pray, and cry aloud, And He shall hear my voice. He has redeemed my soul in peace from the battle that was against me ... Cast your burden on the Lord, And He shall sustain you; He shall never permit the righteous to be moved"*

*(Psalm 55: 1-18, 22, NKJV).*

The worship music droned into a murmur, blending with the whispered prayers of those around me, until I was no longer aware of any sound at all. I was at the altar call, a complete stranger laying hands on my shoulders as I sobbed. Despite her frame being half my size, I was sure her grip was the only thing keeping me from falling to the ground. As tears ran down my cheeks and snot dripped from my nose, I could barely steady my breath to tell her what I needed prayer for. I was humiliated and at rock bottom. I was desperate.

My relationship was failing. For the second time in my life, I was looking at leaving a partner and starting over. At potentially becoming a single mom again. At giving up everything I had worked so hard for. And it wasn't fair. It wasn't fair because it wasn't my fault. It couldn't be; I was doing everything right. And I was telling my partner everything he should be doing right. I was sure the devil had a firm grip on his mental health and no matter what I said or did, it wasn't changing. It was only getting worse. For three years I had watched the love of my life—the father of two of my children—shift and change and transform before my eyes. He was truly a different person—a victim of a deep depression that he could not pull himself out of, and I had no control.

Control. I have always had a profound sense of pride over how busy I am—and how well I do busy. I am a full-time mom, a full-time graduate student, a full-time teacher, a full-time wife, a full-time this, that, and the other. I am busy, busy, busy. I am productive, efficient, and in control of all things around me. Until I absolutely wasn't. And I just couldn't handle it. The loss of feeling in control came with crippling anxiety and fear—not only about what my future would hold but each present day and hour. I needed to keep control to feel safe and secure, but the facade of control I had maintained for so long was running through my fingers like water. Maybe if I threw away the pills, reached out to his family, dumped the booze down the drain, talked his ears off, cried, shamed him, yelled at him, I could get control back. He just had to change. Just drink less! Sleep more! Go to the gym. Just go to therapy, to treatment. Just spend more time with your kids, that will snap you out of it! That's all. And we could be happy again. I had all the answers. But none of it was working, and the helplessness I felt was overwhelming.

So there I was, at the altar call, just begging God to please fix it. Finally doing what I should have done in the first place. . . Giving it to God. I had faced my problems as if I could shoulder them on my own, not calling on God, the only One actually equipped to solve them. But this particular battle was clearly too big for me to carry, a boulder on my back causing me to quake and rendering me unable to hold the pain, fear, and desperation for even a single step further. I was slowly being crushed into the ground. I thought that—like everything else in my life—I could do this alone because I was smart, strong, capable, and independent. I didn't need anyone else or anything else; I could fix the problem myself. Even a problem that truly had nothing to do with me and wasn't my battle to fight in the first place. Even a problem that was a direct attack by the enemy.

Everything I thought and felt was a lie meant to keep me isolated and hopeless. There is no intelligence in believing you can control someone else's feelings and choices—that's irrationality. There is no strength in fighting battles silently on your own—that's isolation. There is no pride to be had about feeling in control—that's an illusion. Irrationality, isolation, and disillusionment are not ways to find victory over anything. In fact, living in this delusion wasn't even hurting the other person who was being directly attacked—it was just further hurting me! Ma'am—the devil is good at his own game. He'll make you believe characteristics that are actually detrimental are your strengths, and this trick does nothing but keep you further from God's purpose for your life. It does nothing but keep you far from the peace you are so desperately trying to grab onto. How can we grasp peace when our hands are so tightly wrapped around our own false sense of control? It is a house of cards.

You see, in the months and years of this mountain getting steeper and higher, not only did I not call on God for help, but I didn't even allow the room for Him to have His hand in it. My thinking was all wrong. My habits were all wrong. I should not have felt pride over how much I could handle, as if the weight of the burden was a trophy. God did not create us to carry things alone. The old adage "God will never give you more than you can handle" is a lie. The truth is that God will never give us more than He can handle—more than we can handle only through Him and by the power of the Holy Spirit. My pattern of thinking that if I could stay busy I could maintain control, and if I could maintain control it made me a strong person was not true. As soon as things got tough, I quickly crumbled under the weight of it and created my own demons of anxiety and depression because my life was, as a matter of fact, very outside of my control. The enemy no longer just had a grip on my husband, he was grabbing a hold of me, too.

As I confided and bared all to this stranger, who so lovingly prayed over me, I desperately listened to her words. She reminded me that the enemy comes to destroy and kill. God comes so that we may have redemption, love, and peace. The broken things in my life were not from a lack of God's love, they were from all the room I had left for the enemy to infiltrate my life and all the room I did not leave for God to intervene. All of those splinters, cracks, and crevices should have been reserved for God, not for myself, and not as space for the enemy. As she prayed my perspective shifted, and I very loudly and clearly heard God say, "It is over." It was powerful, audible, and real. I shook and sobbed. I promised Him at that moment that I would give it to Him. I promised Him that I would focus on the only thing I could truly control—myself. But, girl, if I am being completely honest (which I promised to do), I was terrified. I wanted to believe with every ounce of my being that God truly had this. That He had already won this battle for my family. But I still felt fear that things were too far gone. However, even in that still lingering fear, a weight was lifted from my shoulders, and I forced myself to believe it to be true. I forced myself to walk boldly from that altar call in faith. The one thing I did know was that if there was any chance of things getting better, He was truly the only way. I was going to turn my control into surrender.

\*

In the Parable of the Wise and Foolish Builders, Jesus compares a house built on sand to that built on a rock, much like the house of cards described in this chapter:

> *Therefore whoever hears these sayings of Mine, and does them, I will liken him to a wise man who built his house on the rock: and the rain descended, the floods came, and the winds*

*blew and beat on that house; and it did not fall, for it was founded on the rock. But everyone who hears these sayings of Mine, and does not do them, will be like a foolish man who built his house on the sand: and the rain descended, the floods came, and the winds blew and beat on that house; and it fell. And great was its fall* (Matthew 7:24-27 NKJV).

Rain, floods, and winds are going to come—that is just a fact of life. How will your house stand? Like a house of cards or like a sturdy mansion built into the rock? Reflect on your foundation. What do you need to loosen your grip on, and what do you need to lay fully at God's feet and walk away from in order to strengthen your foundation? As you reflect on my story, think about your own circumstances. Where are you not leaving space for God, but instead creating cracks for the enemy to infiltrate? Write your thoughts below.

_____
_____
_____
_____
_____
_____
_____
_____

I've given some suggestions below on areas in my life that I found I needed to repair to strengthen my own foundation, and I hope this list can serve you as well as it served me.

## People who do not build you up.

Why do we surround ourselves with and sometimes even cater to others that bring chaos and stress rather than joy and peace? Jesus told us to love others, but that is not a call to be a doormat or give ourselves to others in a way that is to our own detriment. Sometimes we may need to leave people where they are, and pray for God's hand to work in their lives. Because—it ain't you sis!—we can't fix all the broken people, that's Jesus' job. Yes, we can lead by example and be a light in this world, and while we can hope that inspires others to follow, we cannot force others into change and we can't drag them with us. Here's the thing, when others see a light and change in you, you are either going to inspire them to come along, or they weren't for the next chapter in your life in the first place. On the other hand, maybe there are certain people who aren't necessarily causing chaos, but a complacent stagnation. Surround yourself with those who build you up and push you to be better. Surround yourself with people who challenge and inspire you. It is so important. As cliche as it is, we really do become like those we surround ourselves with. (We'll talk more about this on Day Eight.) So, are you trying to stay small and stagnant, or big and making moves forward? Crippled in fear and anxiety, or freed into boldness and peace?

Reflect- Who in your life is lifting you up and who in your life may be keeping you anchored in downfall or stagnation? In my own personal testimony, I had to make room for God's hand to work and heal my husband and family. Because I was in a situation that was not serving me or my children in bringing us towards God's bigger purposes for our lives, I had to trust that in releasing control, my husband would follow my lead instead of me trying to drag him along. The point is, don't think that just because someone is currently causing stress or stagnation, you have to add them to a chopping block; but, do be honest with yourself on how to move forward in (or, if appropriate, away from) the relationship. Share your list below:

| My cup fillers, chearleaders, and mentors: | Those causing me stress, chaos, or stagnation: |
|---|---|
| | |

*Situations that cause you anxiety, fear, or stress.*

Now, I am actually a proponent of a healthy dose of anxiety or fear, or more specifically, the act of pushing past that anxiety or fear to overcome and prove to yourself that you can do hard things through Him. This is the exact definition of faith. We need to be mindful in posturing ourselves to function out of a place of faith, not fear. Fear is the weapon of the enemy that leaves us in doubt of God and his promises. We cannot allow fear to undermine our faith. If we are in situations in life that are causing needless anxiety or crippling fear time and time again, we need to reassess where God might be trying to lead us (i.e., what the enemy may be trying to distract us from). Remind yourself: faith, not fear. Yes, I may feel nervous, but my faith in God will get me there. Yes, I may feel anxious, but I have faith that God goes before me and with me. Yes, I may feel unsure, but I have faith in God's promises for my life.

Philippians 4:6-7 tells us, *"Do not be anxious about anything, but in everything by prayer and supplication with thanksgiving let your requests be made known to God. And the peace of God, which surpasses all understanding, will guard your hearts and your minds in Christ Jesus"* (ESV). Pray for God's guidance, and then open your ears to listen! If you are in a job that is causing you stress day after day, maybe it is not the calling for you. If you are finding yourself in relationships plagued with mistrust and stress, maybe God is trying to point you in another direction. Don't make Him drag you kicking and screaming! He won't. Listen to Him and obey. Believe Him for bigger and better things. (We will do a deep dive into this on Day Five.)

Reflect by filling in the table below with things that cause you fear, stress, or anxiety and rewrite them as words of faith.

| What I fear: | What I stand on in faith: |
| --- | --- |
| e.g. rejection | e.g. What God has for me, no one can keep from me. |

## Worldly things that take the focus off of God.

It is so easy to find yourself indulging in "harmless" worldly things. Music, social media, hobbies, and habits can all casually seep, creep, and crawl into the empty crevices of our lives as meaningless ways to cope. If you're anything like me, there is no feeling that a pint of ice cream can't fix— mad, sad, happy, or otherwise. Add a bad reality tv show to the mix? Chef's kiss. There is no situation that angry music can't make me feel just a little bit better about, or that sad music can't make me feel validated in. However, what seems so harmless can lead to some big cracks and holes filled with all of those meaningless things— rather than God's love. These worldly things take the focus off of God. They cause us to rely on things rather than on Him. What we should be praying about, we're stress eating about. When we should be losing ourselves in His Word, we are losing ourselves in that bottle of wine. And where we should be relying on His Love and Grace, we are instead doom scrolling on social media comparing ourselves to worldly influencers rather the greatest influencer of all— Jesus. Now, I'm not insinuating that you need to abandon all of your worldly comforts, invest in a horse and carriage, and don a prairie dress and bonnet, but I am strongly urging you to consider: What do you rely on for comfort and peace and where in your life have you created habits that result in a lost opportunity to spend time with God? God has a future with more blessing, provision, and peace than we can imagine, but that future can only come to pass through healthy spiritual habits that draw us nearer to Him, not farther away. (More thoughts and guidance on this on Day Ten.)

Fill in the box on the next page with some of your most common coping habits:

[ ]

Do these habits draw you closer to or farther away from God?

_____
_____
_____
_____

Fill in the box below with some spiritual habits you can add into your day, or even use as a replacement for your other coping habits:

[ ]

## JOURNAL

Reflect on the tables you filled out above. On a separate piece of paper, notecards, or sticky notes, make a list of all of the things that are currently causing you stress, anxiety, or fear. (If you use a piece of paper, rip it into smaller pieces so each item has its own card.)

Next, sort the items into two piles—things you can control, and things you cannot control. Use each pile to fill out the table on the next page.

With the items you can control, fill in the table by making a list of actionable steps you can take to improve these items—how can you decrease anxiety, fear, and stress, and replace your current habits with spiritually healthy habits that will improve your situation? For example, if you are struggling with physical health, you might consider a healthier diet or taking a walk each evening. If you are struggling with finances, you might consider picking up a financial self-help book, creating a budget, or taking a course.

For the items you cannot control, write ways that you can take a step back, loosen your grip, or even completely hand it over to God. This is where you make room in those cracks and crevices for God to step in.

Think baby steps and goals that are achievable and measurable. In my case, I decided to focus on and spend more time with my children, attend church every single week, and order a book on forgiveness I took up journaling and spent more time in my Bible. I also decided to quit trying to control my husband's choices or actions. I prayed for him, I set firm and predictable boundaries for myself in reaction to his choices, and I decided to show him love but never in a way that could be perceived as enabling.

| Things I can control: | Spiritually healthy habits to improve this area: |
|---|---|
|  |  |

How does your list above compare to how you typically respond to your fears? How might stepping out in actionable faith over fear lead to personal growth? How might giving your fears over to God lead to a deeper reliance on God's strength and guidance in your life?

_____
_____
_____
_____

| Things I cannot control: | How I can take a step back to relinquish "control"? |
|---|---|
|  |  |

Consider the greatest battle you are facing right now. Write a story below that could be your future testimony if you worked towards peace and everything came together for your good:

_____
_____
_____
_____
_____
_____
_____
_____

## PRAYER

*Lord, First and foremost I thank you for this day. I thank you for the air in my lungs and all of your provision. Although I have fears and battles I am struggling with, I recognize that all good things come from You, and I am so grateful for all you do in my life. Jesus, you know the battles I currently face. I pray that you help me to recognize what I need to let go of. Help me to discern what is within my control and what is not. Lord please take my burdens and fears and carry them for me. I lay them at your feet. I can't do it on my own anymore. Please help me to posture myself in faith and not let the enemy distract me with worries, fears, doubts, and stress. I know that I can rest in You and Your promises, and I know your plans for me are greater than I can imagine. Please help me to recognize the open doors you are trying to lead me through. Finally, I pray the Holy Spirit gives me wisdom and guidance as I work through these next ten days to ultimately find a sense of peace that I know can only be found in You.*

*In Jesus' name, I pray,*

*Amen.*

# Day Two

## Mindset: Surrendering My Self-Criticism

♪ Playlist: You Say

*"But you are a chosen people, a royal priesthood, a holy nation, God's special possession, that you may declare the praises of him who called you out of darkness into his wonderful light" (1 Peter 2:9 NIV).*

I'm in the habit of joining Facebook groups for everything. It's actually a running joke in my family and I am often teased, "Oh, did you learn that in one of your Facebook groups?" But the truth is, I love being able to search for groups and find a digital community of like-minded people. Or, sometimes, the groups help me to find a service I may need, suggest tools that might be useful for my current goals, or even teach me how to do some DIY maintenance of my home. Want to meet a group of local ladies who love to read as much as you? There's a group for that. Want some design inspiration for your home, curated to your exact style? There's also a group for that. Need to connect with other women in your current "era"?—yep, a group for that, too. These groups are all organized by characterizations and labels that unify the members: Millennial Mommas, Book Babes, [Insert Your City Here]'s Singles, Budgeting for Beginners...you get the gist. What is so blatantly apparent while scrolling through these groups—or any social media platforms for that matter—is that labels are huge in our society.

Labels—whether based on identity, occupation, status, race, gender, or other factors—can influence our social interactions, opportunities that may come our way, and our sense of self. They play a significant role in shaping our identity through self-perception and even our perception of others. While labels can sometimes help provide clarity or offer a sense of belonging (such as in my beloved Facebook groups), they can also be limiting and divisive. I don't fit there. I don't belong here. I'm not good enough for this. Why is she here? When did he become a part of this, that, or the other? Feelings of division, not belonging, or even invalidation lead to not just a poor self-image, but, even worse—these labels can lead to negative self-talk that often explicitly contradicts what God says about you.

In today's scripture, we are called—or labeled as—chosen, royal, holy, and "God's special possession." However, if you are anything like me—or the 59.3 million other Americans who suffer from anxiety, depression, or any other form of mental health disorder (National Institute of Health, 2024)—it's unlikely that your inner self-talk matches what God has said about you. Too often I go through my day and my internal dialogue involves words such as stupid, not good enough, lazy, lacking, inadequate, weak, ugly—or any other multitude of hurtful words. This is only made worse when the aforementioned social media platforms become the comparison framework for every facet of our lives. There is always someone more– more pretty, more wealthy, more kind, or more intelligent. There is always a page or post just waiting to ignite your inner critic.

Think about it—what labels are you attaching to yourself on a daily basis that go against what God has said about you? Write them in the box on the next page.

While thinking about those labels you've given yourself, let me ask you this—would Jesus talk about you the way you talk about yourself? So often in life, we feel disappointed in ourselves or less than, and it leads to some pretty nasty words that we tell ourselves, and pretty nasty labels that we give ourselves. And these labels ultimately attach directly to our sense of identity. (More on that tomorrow!).

Here is the good news—you are not alone. You are not an anomaly. You are not broken, or miswired, or any other negative label you want to attach to yourself (see how easy that becomes!). While the Bible is filled with beautiful stories of hope, love, and victory, we know it is also filled with people. Real, everyday people just like you and I, which means real everyday people who struggled with depression, anxiety, self-criticism, doubt, and lacking self-esteem.

In Exodus, we see Moses struggle with self-doubt, asking God *"Who am I that I should go to Pharaoh and bring the Israelites out of Egypt?"* (Exodus 3:11). And later, *"Pardon your servant, Lord. I have never been eloquent, neither in the past nor since you have spoken to your servant. I am slow of speech and tongue"* (Exodus 4:10). God has literally called out Moses to be the deliverer of His people, and yet Moses doubts his ability to do so. As if God would mistakenly choose someone unable! Moses pays more attention to what he perceives to be his faults than the fact that God has placed a calling on him, and therefore, he must be a capable leader.

In Judges, we see Gideon also struggle with self-doubt, even though God has called him forward. When an angel of the Lord appears, he greets Gideon as a "valiant warrior" and tells him to "go in the strength you have" to free Israel from the Midianites. Gideon's response is one of doubt and self-criticism: "Pardon me, my lord, but how can I save Israel? My clan is the weakest in Manasseh, and I am the least in my family" (Judges 6:15). The angel of the Lord has labeled Gideon as a valiant warrior with strength, and yet Gideon labels himself as weak and less-than.

Throughout the Bible, we also see Elijah struggling with depression—feeling worthless and alone in the desert, asking for death (1 Kings 19:4) and Job asking God why he "...*did not perish at birth*" (Job 3:11). In Psalms, we see David and others offer words of lament (which, by the way, make up a third of all the Psalms!). Labels such as forsaken, forgotten, rejected, miserable, oppressed, overwhelmed, troubled, alone, fearful, and brokenhearted litter these pages of the Bible, showing the hurt and agony of the writers. No, sis, you are certainly not alone! You are merely an imperfect human who falls into believing the enemy's lies, just as all other humans do.

So, if self-criticism, doubt, depression, anxiety, and negative self-talk are so prevalent within the human condition, what are we to do about it? While we cannot completely avoid negative self-talk, feelings of doubt, or perceiving ourselves to be less than, what we can do is replace this self-talk and actively reflect on, recall, and claim what God says about us. We do this by having an active relationship with God, talking with Him daily through prayer, reading His Word, and reaffirming ourselves of His love for us. We must strive to see ourselves through His eyes, not through the lens of self-criticism or comparison. God reminds us that we are fearfully and wonderfully made (Psalm 139:14), chosen (1 Peter 2:9), and that our worth is not based on perfection, but on His love and grace. We have the means to gain peace from our own criticism and self-doubt because God loves us and considers us His "special possession." And, as if being a special possession, beautifully and wonderfully made, chosen, and loved, isn't a blessing enough, God offers multiple words of affirmation, love, and strength throughout His Word. He also calls us:

## His Child

John 1:12 – *"Yet to all who did receive him, to those who believed in his name, he gave the right to become children of God."*

God calls you His child, adopted into His family through your faith in Jesus Christ.

## Loved

1 John 4:9-10 – *"This is how God showed his love among us: He sent his one and only Son into the world that we might live through him. This is love: not that we loved God, but that he loved us and sent his Son as an atoning sacrifice for our sins."*

God loves us so much that he sacrificially offered up His own Son for us.

## A New Creation

2 Corinthians 5:17 – *"Therefore, if anyone is in Christ, the new creation has come: The old has gone, the new is here!"*

In Christ, God calls you a new creation. Your past is forgiven, and you are made new in Him. Not better, or fixed. But brand new!

## His Masterpiece

Ephesians 2:10 – *"For we are God's handiwork, created in Christ Jesus to do good works, which God prepared in advance for us to do."*

You are God's masterpiece, created with purpose and unique value, ready to fulfill the good works He has planned for you.

## A Friend of Jesus

John 15:15 – *"I no longer call you servants, because a servant does not know his master's business. Instead, I have called you friends, for everything that I learned from my Father I have made known to you."*

Jesus calls you His friend, meaning that you have the choice and ability to have a real and intimate relationship with Him.

## Redeemed

Ephesians 1:7 – *"In him we have redemption through his blood, the forgiveness of sins, in accordance with the riches of God's grace."*

Through Jesus' sacrifice, you are redeemed—brought back from sin and restored to God. Worthy of God's love and adoration. Shiny and new and full of His grace.

## A Citizen of Heaven

Philippians 3:20 – *"But our citizenship is in heaven. And we eagerly await a Savior from there, the Lord Jesus Christ."*

As a believer, you are a citizen of heaven, with an eternal home secured in Christ. Girl, we are just visitors here. Earth is not our home. We have a beautiful heaven awaiting us.

## An Ambassador for Christ

2 Corinthians 5:20 – *"We are therefore Christ's ambassadors, as though God were making his appeal through us. We implore you on Christ's behalf: Be reconciled to God."*

God calls you His ambassador, a representative of His kingdom, tasked with sharing His message of reconciliation. What an amazing calling on our lives as Christians! We are here to spread the Good News to others. Can you imagine crossing the gates into Heaven, knowing you get to bring all of your loved ones with you?

## The Salt and Light of the World

Matthew 5:13-14 – *"You are the salt of the earth. But if the salt loses its saltiness, how can it be made salty again?. . .You are the light of the world. A town built on a hill cannot be hidden."*

God calls you the salt of the earth and the light of the world, chosen to influence and shine His light in a dark world. Again, what an honor it is to know we are here to do God's good works and be a shining light of hope in an often dark world. Hon, you're glowing!

## More than a Conqueror

Romans 8:37 – *"No, in all these things we are more than conquerors through him who loved us."*

You are more than a conqueror through Christ, victorious over all challenges, trials, and difficulties in life—even when it feels hard or scary. You are a CONQUEROR! Flying the banner of Jesus on all of the mountain tops and in all the valleys. How amazing is that!?

## His Temple

1 Corinthians 6:19 – *"Do you not know that your bodies are temples of the Holy Spirit, who is in you, whom you have received from God? You are not your own."*

You are the temple of the Holy Spirit, indwelt by God's presence and empowered for His purposes. Friend—God is literally in you! How could we even begin to be self-critical or doubtful when God finds us worthy enough to dwell within us and work through us?

## An Heir of God

Romans 8:17 – *"Now if we are children, then we are heirs—heirs of God and co-heirs with Christ, if indeed we share in his sufferings in order that we may also share in his glory."*

As a child of God, you are an heir of His promises, sharing in the glory of

Christ. We are not slaves to sin—slaves to our negative thought patterns and perceived shortcomings. No, we are blessed children of God, justified by His grace.

## Blessed

Ephesians 1:3 – *"Praise be to the God and Father of our Lord Jesus Christ, who has blessed us in the heavenly realms with every spiritual blessing in Christ."*

You are blessed with every spiritual blessing in Christ, a recipient of God's abundant grace and favor.

Considering all of these beautiful labels– titles!—that God has bestowed upon us, aren't you grateful that you are who and what God says you are, and not what you perceive yourself to be? Girl, when things get hard and criticism is creeping in, it's important to remember this—you are perfectly crafted in God's image and you are exactly who and how you are meant to be to fulfill God's promises and will for your life. Even when we might have shortcomings, or slip-ups, or a bad day—God already has it all figured out. He has already said who you are. And no one gets to take that from you! Not the enemy, and not yourself. God has said some pretty amazing things about you! And when we fail to remember that, we give into criticism, self-doubt, and maybe even self-loathing, and become a prisoner to those thoughts and are believers of a lie, not God's truth. If Jesus wouldn't talk to you the way that you talk to you, why do you find it okay to talk to yourself that way? Friend, don't believe the lies you tell yourself. Instead, focus on His truth.

## JOURNAL

Part of today's reading mentions Elijah's struggle with feelings of depression. Anyone familiar with the story knows that an angel visited Elijah and offered him rest, food, and water. Wouldn't it be wonderful if all of our woes (self-criticism, depression, anxiety, and fear) could be solved with a snack and a good long nap? While that may not quite be our reality (although it can sometimes help!), here is an exercise to aid you in being more mindful of your negative self-talk and reminding yourself of who you are as a child of God.

Using the list you created, reflect on some of your biggest areas of self-criticism and doubt. What are the labels you give yourself that it is time to ditch? Write these labels on the table below so that you can be more aware when they come across your mind. Now, challenge yourself to look at yourself through God's eyes, instead of your own faulty lens. What are labels God would give you that are contradictory to your own criticisms and doubts? As you become more aware of your self-criticism happening in your own mind, practice replacing those thoughts and labels with what God would say about you!

| Labels I am working to reject: | Labels God would give me: |
|---|---|
| e.g. Not good enough | e.g. I am more than neough, created for God's purpose |
| | |

Today's reading offered many labels, titles, and names that God has called us throughout the Bible, and of course, this was not an exhaustive list. What are some of your favorites and why? Are there other things that God has said about you in His Word that are also your favorites? Or, are there even some that are hard to reconcile with, and why do you think that is so?

___

## PRAYER

*Lord, while I know I am not perfect, I do know I am perfectly designed in your image and with your perfect will in place for my life. I come to you, recognizing the heavy weight of self-criticism that I often carry. I confess that I have allowed negative thoughts and harsh judgments to shape how I see myself. I have been quick to focus on my flaws and failures, forgetting the truth of Your love and the purpose You have for my life. Father, help me to see myself through Your eyes, to recognize my worth as Your beloved child, fearfully and wonderfully made. Replace my self-criticism with Your grace, and teach me to be gentle with myself as You are gentle with me. Holy Spirit, guide my thoughts and renew my mind. Remind me daily of Your truth— that I am forgiven, loved, redeemed, and a masterpiece in God's eyes. Help me to speak kindly to myself, to embrace my imperfections with humility, and to trust in Your strength to carry me through every challenge.*

*Thank You, Lord, for Your love and never-ending grace. I trust that through you, I can move beyond self-criticism and walk in the freedom and peace You have promised me. Please continue to guide me towards peace in my life through your love, grace, and guidance.*

*In Jesus' name,*

*Amen.*

# Day Three

## Identity: Surrending My False Self-Image

♫ Playlist: Who You Say I Am

*"You are the light of the world. A town built on a hill cannot be hidden. Neither do people light a lamp and put it under a bowl. Instead, they put it on its stand, and it gives light to everyone in the house. In the same way, let your light shine before others, that they may see your good deeds and glorify your Father in heaven" (Matthew 5:14-16 NIV).*

I recently chatted with a woman in one of my author groups who, in her previous profession, had been a special education teacher. I took an interest in this as I work with special education students as a school psychologist and, at the time, was just beginning to work toward my dream of writing a book. This woman was already a published author and illustrator, and I appreciated that we shared a similar background, but she was living a dream that I was still striving for. During our conversation, she shared with me that as a child and young adult, she had always dreamed of being a teacher; however, once she obtained her degree and saw that dream come to fruition, it did not take long before she began to doubt whether it was truly what she was meant to be doing. This realization, she confided, left her feeling guilty and even a bit lost. Her lack of fulfillment in who and what she wanted to be for so long left her questioning her identity and purpose. While she did not get extremely specific, I imagine she attached some pretty critical labels to herself. She shared with me that after much back and forth, and a slew of emotions, she fearfully decided to leave her teaching position. "I was terrified!" she shared with me, "But something amazing did come of it, eventually."

Unemployed and focused on building her family, she found herself with more time to explore hobbies and search for what brought her joy. She picked up watercolor painting and also began to explore writing. "These new hobbies reminded me of a childhood dream to one day be an illustrator, and maybe write my own book. But, I was a wife and a mom, not a writer or an artist." She continued to create her art and write in her free time, focusing most of her attention on raising her children. As she shared her love of reading with her children, she felt an increasing call to illustrate and write. Until, finally, years after quitting her teaching job, she cast aside her doubt and self-criticism and stepped out in faith to pursue that dream. Today, she is a successfully published author who has fully written, illustrated, and authored multiple children's books. Her books are illustrated with her own artwork and focus on positive affirmations for children. The most amazing part of this is that through these books, she has been able to reach countless classrooms, libraries, and children. More children, in fact, than she would have ever met face-to-face in a classroom.

God's plans are always bigger than our own! While she felt she had lost an identity in changing paths, it actually allowed God to move her toward a much larger calling where she could impact more children worldwide than she ever could have in a single classroom. All because she ditched the job she didn't love, moved from fear into faith, and realized God's bigger plan for her. A plan she had never dreamed for herself because it was just too big!

As I reflect on my own life, I can see all the identities I've held. Some, I've called myself. Some, I've felt called into. Identities are in a constant state of morphing, changing, and growing. Seasons of life bring new and exciting things, as well as loss and scary things. I want you to take a moment and reflect on some of your own identities, both past and present, and write them below. Which of these have been your favorite? Which ones have you not been quite so proud of?

```
┌─────────────────────────────────────────┐
│                                         │
│                                         │
│                                         │
│                                         │
│                                         │
│                                         │
│                                         │
│                                         │
└─────────────────────────────────────────┘
```

Just like the woman who was so gracious in sharing her story with me, many of us struggle with doubt and self-criticism, attaching labels to ourselves that then become our identity—or what we perceive our identity to be. Look at the identities you aren't so proud of above. Now hear this—the truth is, your identity is not through you, what you have done, or what you will do. Your identity is rooted in what you can do through God by following what He has called you to be. Even when He needs to nudge you ten times before you finally listen! God defines your identity, not you. If the woman in my story had continued to stay on the track she had laid out for herself, rather than stepping out in faith and onto the track God was calling her toward, she would have never realized her much larger calling. She would have never reached so many children had she not shared her talents and stepped into an identity of artist and writer. Imagine what you could be missing out on by not stepping into where God is calling you!

In today's scripture, Matthew reminds us that we are to be a light upon the world. That is, we are to shine and reflect God's beauty and grace into the world. Our identity is shaped by God's grace, love, and the work of Jesus Christ in our lives through the Holy Spirit. Our calling is not based on our perception or the world's standards but on our position as beloved children of God. We should not hide or diminish our light out of fear of what other's responses might be, or what others may call us. While people (including yourself) can speak words and identities that are hurtful, harsh, and sometimes even abusive, God does not. Just as we discussed and reflected on yesterday, God has called us many things—a royal priesthood, a chosen nation, forgiven, raised life, favored individual, called, whole, kings, chosen—none of which are small or limiting titles. Our identity in Christ should be big and bold! Not small and fearful. We must embrace the identity God has given us, not focus on the criticism of ourselves and others. The woman in my story was "not an author" and "not an illustrator" by her own deduction, but through following God's calling she absolutely became both of those things! It's too easy to sell ourselves short. To settle for contentment or just good enough. But God calls us to live an overflowing life of abundance! Not a life of "meh," okay, or good enough. And thank God for that! I know I certainly don't want to be at the end of my life, looking back and thinking, "Meh. That was okay." There are way too many wonderful, exciting, thrilling things to be in this world.

We see a beautiful—and probably the most important—example of a woman stepping into her calling and identity through God in the story of Mary.

*"In the sixth month of Elizabeth's pregnancy, God sent the angel Gabriel to Nazareth, a town in Galilee, to a virgin pledged to be married to a man named Joseph, a descendant of David. The virgin's name was Mary. The angel went to her and said, 'Greetings, you who are highly favored! The Lord is with you.' Mary was greatly troubled at his words and wondered what kind of greeting this might be. But the angel said to her, 'Do not be afraid, Mary; you have found favor with God. You will conceive and give birth to a son, and you are to call him Jesus. He will be great and will be called the Son of the*

*Most High. The Lord God will give him the throne of his father David, and he will reign over Jacob's descendants forever; his kingdom will never end.*

*... How will this be, 'Mary asked the angel,' since I am a virgin?*

*The angel answered, 'The Holy Spirit will come on you, and the power of the Most High will overshadow you. So the holy one to be born will be called [a] the Son of God. Even Elizabeth your relative is going to have a child in her old age, and she who was said to be unable to conceive is in her sixth month. For no word from God will ever fail.'*

*'I am the Lord's servant,' Mary answered. 'May your word to me be fulfilled.' Then the angel left her"* (Luke 1:26-38).

In this biblical account, Mary, a fourteen-year-old unmarried virgin, is told she will bear a child. The angel calls her a "favored" woman. When we look at Mary's circumstances, it would be unlikely that Mary would identify herself as favored. The implications of an unwed mother in this time period would have been detrimental—she could have lost Joseph, her betrothed, been shamed and outcast, and even faced death. But Mary steps into God's calling and the identity He has placed on her, replying to Gabriel that she is the Lord's Servant.

How often do we so willingly and faithfully step into what God has called us to be and do, such as Mary did? Especially when it feels scary or hard. (And especially the first time you are called to do it.) If you're anything like me—not often. If I'm really being honest, maybe not ever. But, as Christians, we must look to what God has said about us! If you don't know what God has said, then you live in the identity of what others have said. And as we've discussed, people can say some pretty brutal and hurtful things. Things that will tear us down. How blessed are we that God defines us, and not anyone else? God speaks over your life and what He speaks is for your good and to build you up. If you do not know who you are or what God has called you, fear will come as a result. Stagnation will come as a result. Feeling and living in less than will come as a result.

- You are a child of God.
- You are favored by God.
- You are chosen by God.
- God is for you.

Your identity in God is deeply rooted in who He says you are, not in your achievements, flaws, or the opinions of others. When we recognize this identity, we can move past fear and into God's favor and calling upon our lives. When we recognize this identity, we move out of discontent and into abundance, fulfillment, and peace.

## JOURNAL

For today's journal exercise, I want you to first take some time to sit in quiet, pray, and listen for God's voice. What are the callings you have put to the wayside based on your fear, self-doubt, and self-determined identity? What areas of your life are you feeling discontent? What identities from your list above do you continue to put on yourself that you shouldn't? What identities have others placed on you? How might these identities contradict what God calls you out to be? What have you failed to do simply because you fear failure or criticism? After taking some time to reflect and pray, write these thoughts down.

_____
_____
_____
_____
_____
_____

## PRAYER

*Dear Lord, thank You for the identity You have given me. Please give me ears and a heart to hear Your true calling on my life. Give me the strength and will to quiet all of the false identities I may limit myself with by listening to what myself and others say, rather than what You have said about me. Give me a heart like Mary's to trust in Your plans for my life so that I may step out of my selfish ways and into what You have called me to be. Allow me to embrace the identity You have given me. Guide me in stepping out from fear and into favor so I can recognize and achieve the calling You have on my life. Please continue to guide me toward peace in my life through Your love, grace, and guidance.*

*In Jesus' name,*

*Amen*

Step 2

# Gratitude

# Day Four

## Moving Out of Fear and Into Favor

♪ Playlist: Good Plans

*"This is what the LORD says: 'When seventy years are completed for Babylon, I will come to you and fulfill my good promise to bring you back to this place. For I know the plans I have for you,' declares the Lord, 'plans to prosper you and not to harm you, plans to give you hope and a future. Then you will call on me and come and pray to me, and I will listen to you. You will seek me and find me when you seek me with all your heart. I will be found by you,' declares the LORD, 'and will bring you back from captivity. I will gather you from all the nations and places where I have banished you, declares the LORD, 'and will bring you back to the place from which I carried you into exile'" (Jeremiah 29:10-14).*

"'For I know the plans I have for you,' declares the Lord, 'plans to prosper you and not to harm you, plans to give you a hope and a future" (Jeremiah 29:11). This verse is probably one of the most well-known and recited scriptures in the Bible. I personally have it on at least two pieces of decor in my home. It has been my go-to when things get hard. My steadfast reminder that God's got me, even when I may not understand what His ultimate plans are or where my struggles are leading me. Jeremiah 29:11 has gotten me through teenage breakups when I felt my heart had been ripped into pieces and later in life through infertility and miscarriage—when it really had been. Despite verse 11 being a favorite, I felt it was important to include the passage in its entirety, as it can be easy for the full meaning to be lost without the context. In this scripture, God is talking through the prophet Jeremiah to the people of Judah who have been exiled into Babylon. The first part of the scripture says *"When seventy years are completed for Babylon"*—meaning, immediate redemption was not in store for the Judeans. However, God does promise to bring the Judeans out of captivity. The message, in its entirety, communicates that even during hard times, God is still with His people and He is working circumstances for greater purposes. Even in our hurt, confusion, bondage, illness, or any other life circumstance, God still fulfills His promises. He has plans to prosper us, help us, fill us with hope, and provide for our future. God promises to pour out His favor on us. That does not mean that what you are going through isn't hard or scary, but that if you maintain a grateful heart you can get through even these circumstances by stepping out from functioning in fear and instead step into God's favor.

But, what exactly is God's favor? Biblical favor can be defined as God's unlimited and unfailing kindness and grace that he bestows upon us. In fact, both grace and favor are the same word in Hebrew—*khen*. Favor is unmerited, meaning we did nothing to deserve it, but it is provided to us because God is a gracious god who loves us. Favor often comes to us as blessings and divine callings from God. This is why it is so important to relinquish control, recognize God's calling on your life and your identity through Him, and maintain an intentional spirit of gratitude. When you can successfully do these things, you leave space for God's will to come to pass. In this space, God will pour His favor out upon you and lead you into blessings, prosperity, and peace, and you will be postured in a way that you are ready to receive it. Allow your life to be what God wants it to be. As we see with the Judeans, that does not mean that there are no hard times, struggles, inconveniences, or discomforts. It simply means that God will work all these things ultimately for your good and His divine will and purpose for your life. And, to be clear, *for your good* does not mean exactly how you want it to play out! Remember, His plans are always bigger and better than anything we can foresee for ourselves.

When we function out of fear, we make choices based on who we are and how little power and control we actually have. This causes us to detour from God's greater purposes for our life. Even when things feel dark, desperate, or hopeless, believe God for big things! Because, bold faith rests on believing in God's power, not our own. In believing the promises He has made. In believing Him. Nothing is too dark, too big, too hopeless for God—nothing is out of His divine reach, so long as we learn to call on Him and lean on Him with big, bold faith! I know, I know. You must be thinking, *But, Britton! You're scared of the dark! How are you going to tell me not to be scared of life?* Okay, you probably didn't even know I am scared of the dark. But, I recognize that this all seems a lot easier said than done. I get it. I've been there. But when we can say yes to what God is calling us into and let go of what God is calling us out of, then we can embrace God's grace that He is extending to us. When we leave this room for God—even in our darkest moments—we can and we will with God and through God. The Bible tells us that all of God's promises are yes and Amen. Amen translates into *Let it be done*. If God can be so faithful, should we not, through our own faithfulness, extend that "yes" back to Him? Just because things are not perfect does not mean that God is not extending His grace. Just because our emotions and feelings might get in the way of the truth—it feels hard, or it feels scary, or it feels like too much—we can still say yes to what God is calling us into, leave at His feet what He is calling us out of, and embrace His calling, grace, and favor upon our lives. Remember! You are not your feelings. You are who God says you are.

Here is how I challenge you to respond when you are in those moments where it just feels too hard, too hopeless, or there is just too much hurt. *"Yes, I will and I can with God."* Being called out of your profession like our friend previously? *Yes, I will and I can with God.* Struggling in your marriage like I was and being called to relinquish control? *Yes, I will and I can with God.* Carrying the burden of loss and depression that feels too strong of a bondage for you to break out of? *Yes, I will and I can with God.* Look at Mary and her yes to Gabriel! It doesn't get much scarier than that. But, you can and you will move from fear into favor by embracing God's calling on your life and the direction He is moving you toward. God is not calling you to feel heavy, burdened, and broken. His purpose for your life is not to be depressed, anxious, addicted, self-deprecating, unemployed, alone, or financially burdened. It is the thief that comes only to steal, kill, and destroy! It is Jesus who came so that we may have life—and have it (drumroll please. . .) abundantly! (John 10:10). Not half-heartedly. Not some. Not a little bit. An *abundant* life is what God is calling you into.

When you switch from stagnation rooted in fear, and move boldly into God's favor by responding *Yes, I will and I can with God* you likely can't even imagine what God will do with that yes! Our minds are small and simplistic compared to God's divine and intricate knowledge of how all the pieces (even the messy ones!) will come together for a greater purpose that we can't envision. Where we have big faith, God can move mountains. But where we have fear and doubt, we can create mountains.

We so easily get stuck on this hamster wheel of life—caught up in an emotion or feeling, functioning out of fear, and becoming frozen because we hold on to what God does not desire for us. Wash, rinse, repeat, and we get nowhere every time. I challenge you to break this cycle. To accept that the battle you are in is not your own but God's. To acknowledge that God has good plans for you. Plans for hope and a future. Plans to prosper. If only you will step away from fear and step boldly into the things that He has for you. Pray to Him. Listen to Him. Focus on His calling in your life, and let go of anything that is not it. Step out in big faith, knowing that you can and you will with God and through His favor.

*On Day One, you wrote down some of your fears. What have you been doing this week to combat those fears? How has that journey been so far?*

_____
_____
_____
_____
_____
_____

In my own story, I absolutely could not see where the struggle in my relationship could possibly be leading me other than to hurt and heartbreak. However, in giving it over to Him and moving out of my fear and into big faith that God could fix it, not only did I receive peace, but my husband was given room to breathe and work toward his own peace. God worked through me, driving me to lead by example and not try and drag my partner along, kicking and screaming. But let's be very real—this was not a passive thing that I did. I did not just hand it over and forget it. I handed over the pieces I could not control and took intentional action in the areas that I could control. In doing so, I saw miracle upon miracle happen in my spouse and healing happen in our relationship. It was not all easy. I often had to recenter, refocus, and remind myself of my *What I can control* vs. *What I cannot control* list. But I will say it was undoubtedly so much easier than going through it with that boulder of burden and a false sense of control on my back. I had peace within myself to let God's will play out for my life. I trusted that if I focused on what I could control, He would do the rest—and that wherever that led, I would be okay. Even if that didn't look like what I was envisioning it to look like. Today I sit here writing a book that I would have never been inspired to write had it not been for that season in my life.

(I do feel like I need a disclaimer here that not all relationships are meant to be healed. God will never call you into being a doormat—to being used, abused, or stuck in a cycle of dysfunction. God does call you out of things. Discernment is where you need to determine and be honest with yourself whether or not God is continuing to call you out, even when you are doing your part to heal. We will talk more about this later on.)

In the table below, list specific problems, challenges, or struggles you see in your life right now. This could be in any area—relationships, finances, business, faith, mental health, etc. In the next column, reflect on if this is something you believe God is calling you into or away from. Is it something you need to learn to embrace or something you need to let go of? Next, list the fear associated with that calling. What is keeping you from moving in big faith, in one direction or another? Finally, write an affirmation to yourself on how you can and will with God's favor.

| The Problem | The Calling | The Fear | The Faith |
|---|---|---|---|
|  |  |  |  |

As we lean into this second step of gratitude, I want you to be mindful of embracing God and posturing yourself towards an actively grateful mindset, even when it's really hard. Specifically, I want you to embrace three things: 1) God's Vision: Really lean into what you discovered in the previous days of how God sees you and what He says about you; 2) God's Works: What God does in your life whether it looks like a problem or a blessing at the time. Not embracing even the hard stuff can be a lost blessing upon you. We will talk about this more tomorrow; 3) God's Plans: Have you caught onto this yet? God has good plans for you. To have gratitude, we must rejoice in God's goodness and be thankful in all things. 1 Thessalonians reminds us, *"Rejoice always, pray continually, give thanks in all circumstances; for this is God's will for you in Christ Jesus"* (5:16-18). This is easy to do when life is going well and things are, well, easy. This is much harder—but even more important to do!—when life is not so easy. Actively practicing gratitude aligns your heart with God's will and allows you to acknowledge all of the good things He has provided, which ultimately brings about peace in any situation. When we can recognize blessings even within the hard parts, we are reminded of God's faithfulness, which directly impacts our mental and emotional peace.

Through active gratitude, we can find assurance of God's love and provision, become more attuned to His presence, and free our minds from the turmoil of life's circumstances. Focusing on problems ignites fear while focusing on the good, God's favor, and our future, ignites hope. We move from fear by no longer focusing on our problems and lack of control, but shifting our focus to God's favor and big power.

## JOURNAL

As we posture our hearts toward gratitude, today's exercise is simplistic and—hopefully!—easy. I want you to remind yourself of all the things you are grateful for. Focus on what God has provided in your life that brings you peace, joy, love, and warmth. These can be big or small, tangible or abstract. When life is feeling yucky, come back to this list to remind yourself of all the wonderful blessings in your life!

I am so grateful and blessed to have:

_____
_____
_____
_____
_____
_____
_____
_____
_____
_____
_____

## PRAYER

*Heavenly Father, I come before You with a heart full of gratitude, acknowledging Your love and Your faithfulness. Thank You for the countless blessings You have already given me. Even in moments of fear and uncertainty, I know that You are with me, surrounding me with Your love and grace. Lord, I confess the times when fear has held me back—fear of the unknown, fear of failure, fear of not being enough. I lay these fears at Your feet and ask for Your strength to overcome them. I know that Your Word says that You have not given me a spirit of fear, but of power, love, and a sound mind.*

*Help me to trust that You are working everything out for my good and that Your plans for me are filled with hope and a future. I invite Your favor into my life, Lord. I recognize that Your favor is not based on my own merit but on Your unmerited grace and love. Thank You for making me Your child and for walking with me through every trial. Your favor surrounds me like a shield, and I trust that You are opening doors, making a way where there seems to be no way, and leading me to a place of victory.*

*As I move forward, Lord, help me to focus on gratitude, even in the midst of challenges. Teach me to see Your hand in every moment and to give thanks in all circumstances, knowing that this is Your will for me. Thank You for Your constant presence, for Your love that casts out fear, and for the favor You pour out on my life. I choose to trust You, to embrace Your goodness, and to walk in the confidence that You are with me every step of the way. Please continue to guide me toward peace in my life through Your love, grace, and guidance.*

*In Jesus' name,*

*Amen.*

# Day Five

## Looking Beyond Discomfort and Inconvenience

♫ Playlist: Hard Fought Hallelujah

"The Spirit of the Lord GOD is on me, because the LORD has anointed me to bring good news to the poor. He has sent me to heal the brokenhearted, to proclaim liberty to the captives and freedom to the prisoners; to proclaim the year of the LORD's favor, and the day of our God's vengeance; to comfort all who mourn, to provide for those who mourn in Zion; to give them a crown of beauty instead of ashes, festive oil instead of mourning, and splendid clothes instead of despair. And they will be called righteous trees, planted by the LORD to glorify him. They will rebuild the ancient ruins; they will restore the former devastations; they will renew the ruined cities, the devastations of many generations. Strangers will stand and feed your flocks, and foreigners will be your plowmen and vinedressers. But you will be called the LORD's *priests; they will speak of you as ministers of our God; you will eat the wealth of the nations, and you will boast in their riches. In place of your shame, you will have a double portion; in place of disgrace, they will rejoice over their share. So they will possess double in their land, and eternal joy will be theirs" (Isaiah 61: 1-7 CSB).*

The Butterfly Effect is a theory that, in essence, demonstrates how small actions can lead to large changes. The theory comes from the idea that the small innocent flap of a butterfly wing can directly affect weather systems across the globe and cause large destructive forces such as tornadoes or hurricanes. According to Britannica Online's "Butterfly Effect: Chaos Theory", this idea is often misunderstood. While people often interpret the Butterfly Effect to mean that they can manipulate or intentionally use certain tools or actions to gain a desired outcome, it is actually a chaos theory. Meaning, there can be no intentionality behind the action that will cause a direct and exactly desired outcome (Rauch 2024). Layman's terms for those who do not pretend to have more than an elementary understanding of math or science like me? X does not automatically equal Z (okay, so maybe that's middle school algebra—but I think you get the gist!). More specifically explained, the butterfly flaps its wings not out of calculated intention, but solely because it is in its nature to fly. It does not flap its wings to cause weather systems to change. The truth of the Butterfly Effect is that a small action may lead to something big, or may, in fact, lead to no change at all (Rauch 2024). Through a Christian lens, we can perhaps interpret the Butterfly Effect, Chaos Theory, or any similar concept to be the divine intervention of God to make order of what is seemingly disorder—all of which works together to serve His plan and purpose for the world and, more specifically, our lives. If we accept this as truth, we must then acknowledge that even in this disorder—the ugly, hard, stressful, or hurtful parts of life, God is ultimately going to work that disorder into order. More simply, God works everything out for good. Romans 8:28 tells us *"And we know that in all things God works for the good of those who love him, who have been called according to his purpose."*

Today's scripture shows an example of this in biblical practice and promise. Once again, we see the Israelites in bondage, with God's promises of the coming of the Messiah that will move the Israelites from bondage to freedom. Because we have been blessed with Jesus' sacrifice, we also are able to move from fear and bondage, to favor and freedom. God restores us. The verse tells us there will be healing for the brokenhearted, liberty for the captives, and freedom for the prisoners. There will be comfort for all who mourn, beauty for ashes, joy instead of mourning, and splendid clothing in lieu of despair. Ancient ruins will be rebuilt, devastations restored, and ruined cities renewed. There will be riches, wealth, and a priesthood. *"In place of your shame, you will have a double portion; in place of disgrace, they will rejoice over their share. So they will possess double in their land, and eternal joy will be theirs"* (Isaiah 61:7 CSB). God is promising to take whatever you have been through, whatever you have lost, and compensate you for it twice-fold. Meaning, that even in the very hard times, we can rest in God's promise that there are bigger and better things ahead for us. Ephesians 3:20 tells us *"Now to him who is able to do immeasurably more than all we ask or imagine, according to his power that is at work within us."* Girl! Do you hear what I am telling you? Do you hear what God is promising? Every bad thing—if we turn to God, if we give it to Him in faithfulness of who He is and what He can do, not who we are and what we cannot do—will not only be turned for good but 👏 in 👏 double 👏 portions 👏! (Handclap emojis are truly the only way to articulate the degree to which I am trying to drive this point home.) He does this in ways that are immeasurably more than we can ask for or imagine! Through comfort, and beauty, and joy, healing, liberty, and restoration, crowns and riches and wealth! How AMAZING is that? Could we ask for better news?

If I look at the trials and tribulations of my life, as well as the victories and successes, I can be certain that every single one led me to exactly where I am today. Like the Butterfly Effect, every small action or inaction appears to have dictated where I ended up. However, from another perspective, every action or inaction may not have actually affected where I've ended up, as it was His divine plan anyway. I may have just added detours in my journey and made it harder on myself along the way. In choosing to do things in my own way, functioning out of fear, or not seeking Him for guidance, I have often failed to leave room for Him and His will or favor. Regardless, I ended up where I was meant to be, once I started believing God for bigger and better; once I placed faith in Him and His promises.

If we believe God creates order out of disorder, we believe that we always end up right where we are supposed to be. It also means that God knows everything that is going to happen in your life—every decision you will make—but He already has a plan in place to bring you through it. Again, if we leave God the space, if we stick to His path rather than our own, our path will be more smooth. Not perfect—this is still the world and this is still life—but better.

Of course, the question is always posed, *Why would God let bad things happen to good people?* Why must these hard times even come to pass in the first place? The answer to this is probably way more complex than I can really cover without a Master of Theology degree. However, what I can gather and put most simply is twofold:

One- God is a good Father. If you are a parent like me (or, if not, reflect on your upbringing) you know that parents can give their children all of the guidance, love and encouragement, mixed with appropriate boundaries and consequences, and even lay out step-by-step plans for them, but kids are still going to do what they want to do—good, bad, or otherwise. It is just an unwritten rule. Kids need to learn from their own choices, even—and especially—from those choices that lead to hurt. As early as toddlerhood, children will take risks that may lead to something uncomfortable—climbing on things only to fall and get hurt, getting into the dog bowl for the third time even though it still tastes just as bad as the first and second time, running too fast and scraping a knee. If my child touches something hot, even after I've told him it is hot, does that mean that I, as a mother, caused him pain? The answer is a simple no. Toddlers, by nature, are curious. They must learn by doing. And as toddlers grow into children and teenagers, the learning just gets a little steeper with harder lessons to learn. While I may not cause any of the bad or hard things that happen to my children, I do allow them to happen to a certain extent. I cannot place my children in a box and shelter them until the day they turn eighteen and then send them on their way. I would be doing them a huge disservice. I would not be allowing them to change, learn, or grow. I would be stunting them from becoming problem-solvers, from building resiliency, and from being able to do hard things without debilitating anxiety or a sense of inability. Just like any other person on the Earth—they have free will and an innate human nature. Although I mother my children the best I can and never wish for any harm to come to them, I must also let them figure it out on their own. I have to allow them to be independent thinkers so that they can grow into—you guessed it— independence. God "parents" in just the same way. He has quite literally given us a manual for our lives, we just often choose not to follow it! He has laid out rules to follow with clearly stated consequences of what happens when we break the rules. Not because he wants to limit or control us, but because he wants us to be happy, healthy, and spiritually sound. But, like children, we choose to do it our own way, which is always the hard way. *Well, well, well,* I find myself thinking far too often, *if it isn't the consequences of my own actions.*

Two- God does not cause the bad things in our lives. God is inherently only good. We often hear It is all part of God's plan, and, while God is all-knowing, meaning he knows the choices you will make, it does not mean that He would have made the same choice for you. It does not mean He planned it for you this way. I would reframe that saying into something more hopeful that is rooted in truth—*God already has a plan for it all.* God already knows how He will pull you out of that mess. He already knows how He will redeem you. He already knows how He will take what you are going through and compensate you two-fold, if and when you are ready to step out of fear and into favor. Just as parents can often help their children learn and grow after a poor decision is made (and they did not heed our advice or guidelines in the first place) God restores us even from our own mistakes. And, yes, sometimes things just happen to us. Not everything is a direct result of our explicit choices; however, evil comes from the enemy. Evil is of the world. Not from God or of God. The world is inherently broken because of sin, and therefore evil is inflicted on us through the world, not through God. The good news is that God's got you. He has a plan for it all.

When we are in hard and even devastating times, we need to remember that God will pull us forward as long as we are willing to shift, stretch, and surrender to Him. We must hold onto God in the midst of our circumstances in order for those circumstances not to become all-consuming. As we discussed on Day One, it's not that God won't give you more than you can handle. It's that situations may arise where it is too great for you to handle without God. Inconvenient and uncomfortable things will unfold in life. It is how we handle it that matters. God cares more about our growth, He cares more about getting us to where He intends for us to be going than he does about us being comfortable in the process. Life is by nature lacking in convenience. But, if we can lean into God as our strength, even the most difficult circumstances become bearable. Not easy, bearable. And eventually, those difficult circumstances lead us directly to where God intends us to be, having more knowledge, faith, strength, grace, and perseverance than we did before we stepped into the battle. We grow through what we go through, so we can find God's purpose in all of it. Because God gave us Christ, we can have a double portion in place of disgrace, hurt, or suffering and eternal joy can be ours (Isaiah 61:7). Because God's already got it figured out, we can rest in the peace of that!

When we consider what it is to be grateful even in our discomfort and inconvenience, we must consider where our focus lies. Are we focused on our fears, doubts, and worries? Or our joys, triumphs, and blessings. As my pastor once described it, when we look back at our previous struggles, we can always have a spiritual 20/20 hindsight of why it had to happen that way.

We can always find the blessings that come out of the burden. Our new perspective, our greater faith, our deepened humility, and our increased patience, all lead to spiritual growth and transformation of our character. Romans 5:3-4 reminds us *"We also glory in our sufferings, because we know that suffering produces perseverance; perseverance, character; and character, hope."* Even more miraculous, this character development can then serve as a ministry. Our struggles allow us a new perspective and greater compassion and empathy for someone who will need it during their tough season, because we have been where they have been, and we have come out on the other side. Much like my hard season in life ended up being the push I needed to step back into my faith, which then led me right here today— writing this book to help others by sharing what I have learned. Mindful gratitude means we recognize God's hand in our life, we acknowledge that only good things come from Him, and we focus on the good, favor, and freedom we have experienced through Him. We focus on the peace we have access to through His grace and promises.

## JOURNAL

One way I find spiritual 20/20 hindsight if I am feeling ungrateful, burdened, stressed, or just stuck is to pause and reflect on where I am now versus six months ago, a year ago, or five years ago. It always puts things into perspective! Like they say, I remember when I used to pray for what I have now. It's so easy to get distracted by the enemy with feelings of inadequacy, fear, hurt, or discouragement, that we forget all of the blessings we have in the now. It's easy to compare ourselves to others or focus on what we have not accomplished, and in that, we lose sight of where we are standing in the here and now compared to where we used to be.

For today's journal, I want you to close your eyes and imagine where you were a year ago. How about two years ago? Or, maybe life has really thrown some curveballs your way recently, and you just need to back it up to yesterday. What blessings and provisions has God given you that you are thankful for today? Where in your life has He given you beauty for ashes? Where have you been compensated with something so much greater than what you lost? What did you pray for that you now have? Write these things down, and revisit them as often as needed to recenter and refocus on how far God has already brought you.

_____
_____
_____
_____
_____
_____
_____
_____
_____
_____
_____
_____
_____
_____
_____
_____
_____

## PRAYER

Heavenly Father,

*I come before You today with a heart that is seeking peace and reassurance. When life feels overwhelming and circumstances seem difficult, remind me that You are always at work, even in the midst of uncertainty. When I can't see the way forward, help me to remember that You are the Creator of all, and Your plans are higher than mine. When life is difficult and I cannot see a way out, remind me that You have already won this battle for me. You already have a plan of redemption, and I need only to leave room for You and rest in Your faithfulness and favor. Help me to keep in the forefront of my mind the assurance that You have already gone before me, preparing the way and working all things together for my good.*

*Lord, grant me the strength to hold on to Your promises and help me to keep my eyes fixed on You. Let my heart be filled with hope, knowing that You are sovereign over every situation and that You are always good, even when I don't understand the circumstances.*

*Thank You for being my constant guide, my provider, and my loving Father. I trust that You have a plan for me and that in every season of life, You are with me, working all things for my good and Your glory. Please continue to guide me toward peace in my life through your love, grace, and guidance.*

*In Jesus' name,*

*Amen*

## Day Six

### Cultivating My Soil

♪ Playlist: Honey in the Rock

*"Then he told them many things in parables, saying: 'A farmer went out to sow his seed. As he was scattering the seed, some fell along the path, and the birds came and ate it up. Some fell on rocky places, where it did not have much soil. It sprang up quickly, because the soil was shallow. But when the sun came up, the plants were scorched, and they withered because they had no root. Other seed fell among thorns, which grew up and choked the plants. Still other seed fell on good soil, where it produced a crop—a hundred, sixty or thirty times what was sown'" (Matthew 13:3-7).*

Soil, seed, and crops are images we often see repeated throughout the Bible. The idea of crops is used metaphorically and literally in both the Old and New Testaments, within both stories and parables. We have all heard "You reap what you sow," "A good tree bears good fruit," and "Casting your seed." As early as Genesis, we see the importance of the ground—or soil—in the story of Cain and Abel. When Jesus speaks to His disciples in the Gospels, He uses the Parable of the Weeds and the Parable of the Sower to teach that good soil produces good crops. But what is "good soil" exactly? How do we reap what we sow? What are we even sowing? These latter two questions are important to ask yourself. While the first question—what is good soil—has a specific answer, the latter two questions may vary for each person. What I reap and sow may be much different from what you reap and sow, and is dependent on the quality of our soil. The soil is our life. It is our heart, mind, and spirit. It is our ability to hear what God has for us and see what God sees in us. It is our ability to understand God, His goodness, and the power of the Holy Spirit. If we want good things to come out of our lives, we have to have good soil. If we want to reap a good crop—that is, have a Holy Spirit-filled life, we must have a good and healthy mind, heart, and spirit for that crop to grow out of!

Have you ever known someone who just seems to have bad things happen to them over and over again? When I think of such people, a childhood friend comes to mind. This girl has made poor choices since I met her in high school, throughout our young adult lives, and even today her decision-making is questionable. My friend was often in trouble in high school—sneaking out, drinking, and hanging out with older kids she had no business hanging around. As we grew up, she did not have a clear direction for her life or what she wanted to do. She was stuck in jobs that brought her no sense of purpose, and in relationships that were harmful to her physically, emotionally, and mentally. She lost cars due to not being able to make the payment, personal belongings to "friends" who would steal from her, and was used and abused within her circle due to the people she chose to surround herself with. As a friend, watching it was just painful. Eventually, I had to step away from this friendship.

Today, this friend has multiple children with multiple men, does not have a career, and struggles financially, physically, and mentally. To be clear, I do not share any of this to shame or ridicule this person. (Quite the opposite; I love her, and my heart hurts for her because I know the freedom and peace she could experience if she would turn to Jesus.) But, I do share this story because the biggest thing that weighed on our friendship wasn't even her poor choices—it was her response to the result of those choices. She just couldn't seem to realize why bad things always *happened* to her. From my perspective, those things didn't happen to her. She created situations and relationships that put her in a bad position. She made choices that led to hard consequences. And all of these things only exacerbated her predicament because she always looked at herself as a victim. Her locus of control was completely external—meaning, she perceived things to be happening to her at all times, rather than a belief that she was in control and could affect change in her own life. The soil of her life was a mess! Her life did not produce good fruit or good crops because she did not lay the proper groundwork. She did not care for her soil. She was reaping what she was sowing, and it was causing her misery, which also made others around her miserable from her constant negativity and outlook on life. This is exactly what God does not want for us, and likely why the Bible is so repetitive with the use of this metaphor. God does not want this message to be lost upon us! He does want us to be living an unfulfilling and purposeless life, much like my friend is experiencing.

In the parable from today's scripture, Jesus describes four types of soil. The first is soil along the walking path, the second is soil in a rocky place, the third is soil among thorns, and the fourth is good soil. When we consider what the soil in our lives represents, we know that Jesus is specifically referring to our ability to hear and see what God is saying and showing to us—do we have a mind ready to hear, a heart ready to listen, and a spirit ready to be filled? Good soil allows us to see with our eyes, hear with our ears, and understand with our hearts (Matthew 13:15). We need to tend the conditions of our mind, body, and spirit (the soil) in order to receive and gain discernment in God's Word (the seed), and fulfill His calling and purpose for our life (the crop). This is where we get "You reap what you sow." The crop of your life is directly related to what you sow into it, and bad soil does not allow the sowing of good seeds or the growing of good crops.

We can think of it this way. How many times have you made a resolution for change? This may have been a New Year's resolution or just a goal you have set for yourself. (New Year, New You! Well... at least for a couple of days, anyway.) Now think of how many times you've been successful in these resolutions and what set you up for either success or failure. We can look at the success or failure of these resolutions in the same four ways Jesus describes the soil:

1) Soil Along the Path- A friend texts you and asks you to start going to the gym with her four days a week. You are so overwhelmed that even thinking about adding a workout to your calendar is too overwhelming. This is like the seed that has fallen along the path—there was no soil there to gather the seed, and so there is no yield. You were not mentally in a place to take on a new habit and therefore did not want to consider it. Your mind wasn't ready.

2) Rocky Soil- You decide you are going to start going to the gym four days a week. You write down some weight loss goals and hit the ground running. Week one you are all in! Week two is a little harder but you still get yourself there. Week three you are down one pound, frustrated with your lack of progress, and give up completely. This is the rocky soil—as soon as things got a little tough (the sun) you gave up (the scorched plants). Your spirit was downcast and frustrated.

3) Soil Among the Thorns- You decide to go to the gym four days a week. You have a set plan of how, when, and why. You are doing great, but your friends pressure you into skipping *just this one time*—the invites to go out to eat, indulge in that sugary coffee you've sworn off, or skip the gym for a social event eventually trump sticking to your plan. This is the soil with the thorns—your plan was thwarted by the environments you put yourself in. Your heart wasn't in it.

4) Good Soil- You've decided to work out four days a week. You have a set plan of how, when, and why. You have shared your plan with those around you and asked them to help hold you accountable. You have set

firm boundaries on what you will indulge in and what you will not, what your schedule looks like, and you have a plan in place for social events. You are disciplined and stick to your plan. You meet your goals (the crop). This is like the good soil of the parable. You have a mind, heart, and spirit open and committed.

Think about these metaphors in relation to your life—no, it does not need to be specific to the gym! I don't like to think about the gym either. How is your mind, heart, and spirit postured towards God? What areas could you work on and what could that look like for you? Write your thoughts in the box below.

When we consider my high school friend, what changes would she need in order to have good soil, seed, and crop? Honestly, the exercises earlier in this book would probably be very helpful for her! Our soil consists of everything not only inside of us but also around us because everything around us can affect everything inside of us. Who we surround ourselves with, what we consume in entertainment and social media, the books we read and the podcasts we listen to, all of these things can bring us either closer to God or farther away from Him. All of these things can create good, healthy soil or poor soil, depending on the content and how it lifts our spirits, fills our hearts, and affects our minds. My friend would need an overhaul of what is around her and what is within her, to have good soil prepared for good seed, which would eventually show in her life through good crops.

By accepting Jesus and moving out of fear and into faith, she would move from an identity of being a victim of circumstance to recognizing her true identity as a redeemed child of God who is blessed and walking in His favor.

What does this parable mean for us when we consider fear, anxiety, or lack of peace? When you do all of the things we have been working on the last few days—leaving room for God, moving from fear into faith, understanding your identity in Christ, recognizing God's favor in your life, and practicing gratitude in all seasons—you are tilling your soil. This is an ongoing process that is intentional and so important. This is also a process that can be so difficult when there are so many thorns in the world and in our circumstances. While the culture we create for ourselves can tend our soil, the soil of our life also becomes the culture we create for ourselves. It is a circular process and a cycle that can only be broken or maintained through intentional action. When we move into an even broader scope of not just our personal culture, but that of our society and world? Yikes! Safe to say the world is perhaps the most politically and socially divided it has ever been. How do we tend our self-culture with the infiltration of the country and world's culture?

Many theologians and scholars refer to many aspects of today's culture as *Cain Culture*. As we know, Cain killed his brother Abel due to jealousy and not following God's commands and guidance. When the Lord asks Cain where Abel is, Cain replies that he does now know. *"The LORD says to Cain, 'What have you done? Listen! Your brother's blood cries out to me from the ground. Now you are under a curse and driven from the ground, which opened its mouth to receive your brother's blood from your hand. When you work the ground, it will no longer yield its crops for you. You will be a restless wanderer on the earth'"* (Genesis 4:10-12). The word *ground* is used three times in this short passage. The ground—quite literally—is Cain's soil. His soil has been stained by his sin and his brother's blood and God condemns the soil to no longer yield a crop.

Cain Culture directly comes from this story as it refers to a culture of jealousy, lack of accountability, violence, and estrangement from God. With our society being inundated by comparison through social media, false standards of perfection, entitlement, social and racial division, an affirmation culture that is rooted in feelings and emotions rather than truth, and every tool of the enemy being used to wipe God out of our society, the direct tie between Cain Culture and today's modern society becomes quite clear. A Cain Culture leads to some pretty gnarly soil– forget just birds, rocks, and thorns. I envision a desert overgrown with long-dead shrubbery and some pretty sketchy creatures creeping, crawling, and slithering around. Not a great setting for a fruitful crop!

So, how do you tend your own culture and soil in order to receive what God has for you? If we look at God's biblical law and the example Jesus set for us, neither of these things aim to limit us but to free us. It is all intended to prepare our soil. By rejecting worldly and selfish things, and accepting spiritual law and practice, we can better tend our soil. Proverbs 4:23 tells us *"Guard your heart above all else, for it is the source of life"* (CSB). We must protect our hearts, minds, and spirits in order to tend our soil and be receptive to God's Word and calling on our lives. In doing so, Jesus tells us we will produce a crop a hundred, sixty, or thirty times beyond what we've sown into it (Matthew 13:23).

With a grateful heart, we can maintain our good soil. In Hebrews, we are reminded that through Jesus' sacrifice, we have sprinkled blood that speaks a better word—a new covenant—than that through the blood of Abel (Hebrews 12:24). Keeping our eyes focused on the good of the world and the blessings that God has provided us, we can maintain a spirit of gratitude and tend our soil so that it does not become overgrown with other worldly stressors that can create toxic soil, seed, and crop. A culture rooted in Jesus offers us hope for restoration! This good soil will give us good ground to practice our own grace and forgiveness, which will lead to personal, relational, and spiritual peace.

## JOURNAL

In the parable, Jesus describes three different types of soil. In reflecting on your life, how would you describe your soil currently? How is the condition of your heart, mind, and spirit? Is it rocky, leaving you easily influenced and discouraged by the world? Is it thorny and you need to reevaluate the environments and relationships you find yourself in?

_____
_____
_____
_____
_____
_____
_____
_____
_____

What changes can you make in your life to better prepare your soil? Are there things in your personal culture you need to rid yourself of? Relationships you need to take a step back from? Or maybe things you need to add to your day-to-day life in order to tend your soil and strengthen your heart, mind, and spirit.

_____
_____
_____
_____
_____
_____
_____
_____
_____

# PRAYER

Dear Lord,

First and foremost, thank You so much for this day. Thank You for the blood of Christ Jesus that allows us a new covenant. Please guide me in protecting my heart and mind from worldly influences that can lead to rocks and thorns in my soil, making it more difficult to discern your call and purpose for my life. Allow me to see with my eyes, hear with my ears, and understand with my heart. Lord, I recognize that just as a farmer must prepare the soil to receive a bountiful harvest, I must also prepare my heart to receive Your Word.

I ask You to help me cultivate good soil within me—soil that is soft, receptive, and ready for Your truths to take root. Remove any hardness or distractions that might hinder my growth, and help me to nurture a heart that is open to Your will. Please continue to guide me toward peace in my life through your love, grace, and guidance.

In Jesus' Name,

Amen.

Step 3

# Grace

# Day Seven

## Grace for Self: Seeking Personal Peace
♫ Playlist: God Really Loves Us

*"Come to me, all who are weary and burdened, and I will give you rest. Take my yoke upon you and learn from me, for I am gentle and humble in heart, and you will find rest for your souls. For my yoke is easy and my burden is light" (Matthew 11:28-30).*

I've noticed a new trend on social media lately. Normal, everyday people are pushing back against the unattainable image that influencers present. In fact, some influencers have even followed along, showing the "real" parts of their lives. This trend is often presented with titles like "Tour My Nonaesthetic Home" and includes hashtags such as #NonaestheticMom or #RealisticLifestyle. If you spend even a portion of your day on social media, you know that the struggle is real when it comes to not comparing yourself to others. Too often we get stuck in feelings of inadequacy all because we are stuck in a pattern of comparison—most of the time to people we don't even actually know! At no other time in our history has Keeping Up With The Joneses, or The Kardashians, or [insert influencer's name here]been so in our faces on such a constant and unrelenting basis. It can be easy to compare ourselves to the very unrealistic reality that people choose to show on social media, making us feel envious and inadequate.

*Well, the Johnsons got a new vehicle, so why shouldn't I?*
*How did the Smiths afford another vacation?*
*I need to DIY reno my kitchen, immediately.*
*Becky got another promotion?*
*Look at all of her friends! I'm so jealous of her social life.*
*I work hard; I deserve all of these things too!*
*She is just so blessed and close to Jesus, I wish my spirit was filled like hers.*

As if life doesn't present enough challenges that could easily wear us down, we add to that load by holding ourselves to unrealistic expectations of what life should look like according to @BlessedMommaLifeIsPerfectEverythingIsWonderfulAllTheTime. This comparison just creates a negative self-image that is actually a lie. It leads to a feeling of complete unrest and personal burden. We are constantly trying to reach a bar that is not only too high, it just doesn't actually exist. It is not real life. How can we ever feel at peace if we are constantly chasing a nonexistent target?

In today's scripture, Jesus invites us to come to Him with our burdens and to experience rest. This does not mean that we have to be guilt-free or perfect to come and bring our burdens to Him. It means if we are tired, weary, drained, stressed, or disappointed, we can bring all of these things to Jesus, and not only will he show us grace, but we can give ourselves grace by acknowledging our need for rest and peace. God is our soft spot we can fall on when we are just too tired to do it ourselves. We do not have to have it all together to earn God's love and grace. Remember, it's unmerited! So, if God can show us grace and mercy, we need to be humble enough to show it to ourselves. Too often, we are our own worst critics. Remember your self-proclaimed labels and identities you wrote down on Day Three? We know that Jesus would not talk about us the way we talk about ourselves. So often, our negative self-image and lack of personal peace stem from three things: 1) mistakes we have made; 2) failures we've experienced; and 3) comparisons to others.

## Mistakes We Have Made

**The lies:** The mistakes I've made are too great to forgive. They have brought me too far from God to ever recover. I need to overcompensate for what I've done in the past.

**The truth:** God has already forgiven you. God is always waiting to welcome you home. It's His heart's desire that you should find salvation and remain close to Him (1 Timothy 2).

When we consider mistakes we have made in our lives, how do we move past the hurt it has caused us or others? The answer is this: we must give grace to ourselves, just as God has given it to us. We must humble ourselves to know that God has already forgiven us and has moved on, and we must do the same. When we make decisions that do not align with our values, it does not make us bad. It makes us confused. It makes us human. It simply means we have erred by functioning out of fear or anxiety, rather than functioning out of God's peace and promises. You have never messed up so big that God cannot forgive it or fix it! You do not need to go above and beyond to try and right every wrong you have ever committed. You need only to bring it to Him, request His forgiveness, align your heart with Jesus, and move forward. You must forgive yourself, just as He has forgiven you.

## The Failures We've Experienced

**The lies:** I'm just not good enough. I can't recover from this.

**The truth:** We are God's perfect creation (Genesis 1:31), made in his image (Genesis 1:27), and no matter how many times we fail, we will always have redemption (Proverbs 24:16).

Proverbs 24:16 tells us that even if we fall and fail seven times, we will rise again. When we have a dream that doesn't come to fruition, a job we haven't found success at, or a relationship that didn't work out, we are often overly self-critical. We can get so hyper-focused on our shortcomings that we umbrella-term our way into false identities or fall into a victim mentality—both of which can be crippling to our growth and chance of future success. In these times we should be diving into the truth delivered by scripture, rather than believing the enemy's lies. Step out of your bondaged way of thinking, for God has already broken the chains that we so often put on ourselves (Psalm 107:14). We must move from a spirit of *Woe is Me* to *Greater is He*. Instead of telling yourself *I'm not good enough*, live in the biblical truth that *God has created me with intention*. Instead of *I was dealt a bad hand*, walk in the truth that *no matter what cards I was dealt, I've already won the game because God has already worked it out* (Romans 8:28).

## Comparisons We Make to Others

**The lie:** She is doing so much better than me; I wish I had those blessings.

**The truth:** God does not show favoritism (Romans 2:11). What He has done for others He can also do for you.

The enemy would have you believe that everyone is out there doing better than you. That God is just giving them a fruitful life with blessing upon blessing through some sort of spiritual disparity. It is a lie not only for the fact that, well, they're probably not truly doing better than you but only showing you the pieces they want to share, but also for the fact that the ground is level at the foot of the cross. We don't see the credit card debt they've wracked up, the closeted alcoholism that is plaguing their relationship, or the strained relationships with their children due to long hours at the office. Every single person faces battles in life. For all things, there is a season (Ecclesiastes 3:1). Just because someone else is in a different season than you, does not mean you know what they have gone through to get there. But what we do know is that even if they aren't in a season of trial and God is pouring out His blessings and favor upon them in a season of fruitful harvest, God can do that for us, too. The truth that refutes the lie is that God is never doing anything for anyone else that He cannot also do for you! You need to tend your own soil to produce the crop you are looking for.

Which of these lies resonated with you the most? What comparisons are you making or shortcomings are you allowing to hold you back? What steps can you take in your life to feel satisfied and at peace with your circumstances?

_____
_____
_____
_____
_____

Despite mistakes, shortcomings, or self-criticism you are not defined by your past or your current circumstances. A difficult past does not make you any less worthy of God's grace and favor. A difficult present does not mean it is okay to fall into an envious spirit that keeps you in a Woe is Me mentality. What is done is done. 1 Corinthians tells us that love keeps no record of wrongs (13:5). Love yourself enough to let go of what has weighed you down in the past because God loves you that much. God has more for you in your future. Your past has nothing on you because what God has for you is not behind you but in front of you! Why are you looking behind you when God is calling you forward? God gives us hope for a future, not for the past.

Do not dwell on what is already dead. There is *new life* in you through Christ. Did you catch that? Made new. Not fixed, or better, or less bad—brand new. God tells us in Isaiah 43:18-19 to forget the former things, because He is doing a new thing. If God is not dwelling on our past mistakes, why would we? If God has sufficient grace, who are we to withhold that grace from ourselves? Never be so proud that you believe your word stands over God's, or that you should be more critical of yourself than God is. Extend to yourself the same grace and forgiveness you would extend to others, and that God would extend to all of us. That, my friend, is where you will find personal peace with who you are and where you are going.

Common lies we may tell ourselves about why we do not deserve forgiveness or grace may sound something like:

*I just don't deserve it.*
*What I did was too terrible to forgive myself.*
*I've caused too much damage to myself and others to ever move forward.*
*I should be better than that.*
*I know better than what I did, and I did it anyway. It's my own fault.*

Have you told yourself any of these lies? What would you add to this list?

___
___
___
___
___
___

Even as a new creation in Christ, we are still human beings, and we need to have expectations as such. News flash—we have messed up before and we will mess up again, no matter our best intentions. It is our nature as human beings, even when we wish it wasn't. Paul writes in Romans 7:21-25 *"So I find this law at work: Although I want to do good, evil is right there with me. For in my inner being, I delight in God's law; but I see another law at work in me, waging war against the law of my mind and making me a prisoner of the law of sin at work within me. What a wretched man I am! Who will rescue me from this body that is subject to death? Thanks be to God, who delivers me through Jesus Christ our Lord!"*

Paul is describing the human experience as all Christians experience it—an internal war between our flesh (nature) and our spirit. But, as Christians, we know that even when we make mistakes and sin, we have grace and freedom, all because Jesus came and paid the ultimate price for us. His grace is sufficient. His blessings are abundant! I will say it again—there is nothing He has done for someone else that He cannot also do for you. You have the ability to not only seek out but fiercely pursue a relationship with God. You have the means to tend your soil, plant good seed, and yield a good crop. God is for you, not against you. God wants you to have life and have it abundantly! There is nothing you have done to make that impossible, and there is nothing you could do to make it untrue. Seek first the Kingdom of God and all else will be given to you! (Matthew 6:33). You don't have to worry if you are worth it, or if you deserve it. It is not about who you are, it's about who He is. You can have peace with yourself knowing that you are fearfully and wonderfully made (Psalm 139:14), you are loved (John 3:16), you are enough, and if God is for you, who could be against you (Romans 8:31)—including yourself? Our mistakes do not define us! God's love and grace do.

## JOURNAL

Sit in a quiet space, close your eyes, and think of some of the moments of your life that came to mind to you during today's reading. Moments when you felt burdened by self-criticism, failure, or comparison. I want you to write those moments down below:

_____
_____
_____
_____
_____
_____
_____
_____
_____

How have those thoughts above impacted your peace and joy?

_____
_____
_____
_____
_____
_____
_____
_____

Now, I want you to take each of the things you wrote above, and individually and audibly give yourself grace for each and every one. Surrender it to God. Out loud, remind yourself that these are things of your past. These are not things that God has for your future, therefore, they are not things that should hold weight in your future. Do you have a Woe is Me spirit about these things? How can you move into a Greater is He mindset? Say it out loud. Release it all, once and for all, and then step forward in faith, leaving these things behind you.

Finally, I want you to come up with an actionable plan of how you will extend grace to yourself in the upcoming week. It might be having a bible verse that resonates with you that you will reread, a song you might listen to, or a creed you might repeat. What will this look like for you:

_____
_____
_____
_____
_____
_____
_____
_____

## PRAYER

*Dear God,*

*Thank You for Your infinite love and grace. I come before You, recognizing the burden of self-criticism, failure, and comparison that I carry. Lord, I often find myself focused on my shortcomings, measuring my worth by standards that aren't Your own. Help me to see myself as You see me—loved, cherished, and enough just as I am. Give me a heart more like Jesus, where I can freely extend grace to myself as He did to others.*

*Grant me the grace to forgive myself for past mistakes, to release the weight of comparison, and to embrace Your tender mercy. Teach me to walk in the assurance that You are with me, guiding me through each step of growth.*

*Help me to offer myself the same love and understanding You give so freely, trusting in Your plan and timing. I place my heart in Your hands, knowing that with You, I am always enough.*

*In Jesus' name,*

*Amen.*

Step 4

# Forgiveness

# Day Eight

## Forgiveness of Others: Seeking Relational Peace

♫ Playlist: Chain Breaker

*"Get rid of all bitterness, rage and anger, brawling and slander, along with every form of malice. Be kind and compassionate to one another, forgiving each other, just as in Christ God forgave you" (Ephesians 4:31-32).*

Who has hurt you? Who has lied to you? Has anyone lied about you? Who betrayed you, belittled you, or caused you to feel small or inadequate? So many times in life, we are hurt and betrayed by others. Often, it is the people we are the closest to that cause us the most harm. The poet, William Blake, wrote an entire poem about it, entitled "It is Easier to Forgive an Enemy Than to Forgive a Friend." It is far easier to be hurt by someone we love because we have expectations of them. We expect our friends to love us back, not to hurt us. We expect an enemy to hurt and deceive, we do not expect that of our loved ones. But unfortunately, hurt comes from loved ones as well—whether they intend it or not. How do we forgive these people that have hurt us the most? I don't know about you, but typically, when I hear the word forgiveness, I cringe a little. Like, okay, if you accidentally stepped on my foot, I'm going to be pretty quick to forgive you! But what about those deep hurts and pains? The wounds we can't see? The loss that is just too great? Forgiveness just feels too hard.

Depending on the translation used, the Bible contains the word *forgive* or *forgiveness* up to ninety-five times. To forgive is a direct commandment. It is not a suggestion or something to consider. So, if God has told us to forgive, wouldn't it be nice to know *how* to forgive? To be given a step-by-step manual? I mean, you want me to forgive, God, I get it. But how do I forgive when I am hurting so deeply? Why would I want to forgive, when what they did was so horrible? The truth about forgiveness is that—although it might be a word that makes us cringe—it is an action that is actually a gift from God. And, I'm not talking in the sense that it's a gift to us that He forgives us—I'm talking in the sense that it's a gift to us to be able to forgive others. But, that doesn't mean it's not complicated to try and understand how to forgive, or even what forgiveness means. But it is important to learn how and what—because forgiving those who have wounded us the deepest, is a grace we can give to *ourselves*.

In my own story, I remember so clearly not knowing how I could possibly forgive my husband for the hurt he had caused. I wanted to. I wanted to move forward. But I had so much fear and pain holding me back. What if I just get disappointed again? What if he does the same thing to hurt me again? *I'm too angry to forgive him anyway, even if I do want to!* Forgiveness may feel impossible. The hurt might be too fresh or too deep. Your anger might be too great. And many people may truly not even care to have your forgiveness! They may not be deserving of it from you. (*I'll leave it between them and Jesus!*) But here is the thing—it's not about what they deserve, it's about what you deserve.

I want you to think about who you have been holding out on forgiving. In the box on the next page, I want you to write down every single emotion that person made you feel, and every single feeling you have about them.

Now, look at those words. Those emotions and feelings—those are things you are carrying in your heart and soul. Those are emotions that you are burdened with. They are not things that are hurting the other person; they are things that are hurting you. You do not have to pick up what someone has done to you, sling it over your shoulder, and carry it with you every day. You can put it down. That is what forgiveness does. That is why forgiveness is grace unto yourself. The person who hurt you cannot heal you. They may have caused the pain, but they cannot cause the healing and restoration (even if they are truly sorry, and certainly not if they aren't sorry at all). But do you know who can heal your pain? You. . .with God working through you and in you. God forgives us and extends grace to us, and through that, we can extend forgiveness and grace to others. But, let's be sure we know what forgiveness is—and is not.

## Forgiveness Is:

1. Forgiveness is something that must take place through active cooperation with God. When we have messed up, sinned, and went against God, He forgives us anyway, so who are we to deny forgiveness to others? God's forgiveness and grace comes to us, works through us, and allows us to extend it outward to others. This does not mean we are perfect in this process, but that we are making a decision to actively

pursue being more like Jesus, and cooperate with God in the process. We are commanded to forgive as the Lord forgave us (Colossians 3:13) If we are to truly lean into God's will and favor upon our lives, we must cooperate by following His commands.

2. Forgiveness is a weight and burden off of you. Remember, you are the person carrying around those emotions and feelings of bitterness, resentment, anger, and any other word you wrote in the box above. Those feelings affect your heart and spirit, not the heart and spirit of the other person. A heavy heart makes us easy to anger and gives us a sharp tongue. You can never find rest and peace when your heart and spirit are inundated with feelings of unrest and anger. This keeps us farther from God (James 1). Instead, forgiveness is a freedom and grace that gives us a light heart and gentle spirit, which keeps us closer to God.

3. Forgiveness is letting go of your own sin. Today's scripture tells us to get rid of anger, rage, bitterness, brawling, slander, and malice. If we hold on to these things, we are unable to be freed from them. They remain a shackle and chain holding you down and keeping you farther from God. Time and time again we are told in the Bible to not be bitter but to live in peace and with kindness and grace. How can God release our shackles and chains if we are unwilling to do so for ourselves?

## Forgiveness is Not:

1. Forgiveness is not weakness. Forgiving is not an option we're given. It's a command from God. Meaning, we have to do it even when we feel like we don't want to. Forgiving something that's been done to you or someone that has hurt you is not being weak. It shows spiritual maturity and grace. It is not our job to bestow some sort of punishment or consequence on those who have wronged us. *"Do not repay anyone evil for evil. Be careful to do what is right in the eyes of everyone. If it is*

*possible, as far as it depends on you, live at peace with everyone. Do not take revenge, my dear friends, but leave room for God's wrath, for it is written: 'It is mine to avenge; I will repay,' says the Lord"* (Romans 12:17-19). We need to free ourselves from feeling responsible for creating consequences for those who have hurt us and give it to God to handle so that we can walk forward in peace.

2. Forgiveness is not justification or a lack of boundaries. When we forgive someone it does not mean we accept what they did as okay or right. It does not mean we condone or enable. It also does not mean that we have to change our boundaries or what we are willing to accept from those we have relationships with. In fact, arguably, forgiveness could even be looked at as a healthy boundary; when you forgive, the chain or bondage holding you to that other person is severed and gone.

3. Forgiveness is not reconciliation. While forgiveness can open the door to reconciliation, reconciliation is not a mandatory component of forgiveness. We do not have to reconcile with unhealthy, abusive, or harmful people. In fact, God tells us not to bind ourselves with others who do not align with our values and beliefs (2 Corinthians 6:14).

Considering the list above of what forgiveness is and is not, which do you struggle with the most? Which offer you the most clarity and hope?

_____
_____
_____
_____
_____
_____
_____
_____

Once we have a better understanding of what forgiveness is and is not, we can then look at what a lack of forgiveness does to us, so that we can answer why we must forgive. We know God told us to, but we also know it's hard. Why would God command something of us that is so difficult? We know that God loves us and wants good things for us; therefore, we know that if He commands us to forgive, it must be for our own benefit.

When we hold on to anger, resentment, hurt, and grief, they take a toll on our heart and spirit. These emotions boil and seep and crawl into every crevice of our being, becoming all-consuming. Proverbs 4:23 warns us, *"Above all else, guard your heart, for everything you do flows from it."* If our heart is full of bitterness and resentment, we can be sure that what is flowing from it is also bitterness and resentment. This turns our words harsh and critical, our outlook cynical, and makes our spirit tired and mean-spirited. None of these things have any real impact on the person who hurt us. Instead, we are allowing their actions to cause continuous hurt and even spiritual distress. In reality, all you are doing through unforgiveness is allowing the person who hurt you even more power to continue hurting you. This is what the enemy desires for you while God desires for you to be free. The enemy hopes to keep you in the bondage of unforgiveness through depression, anxiety, substance abuse, family breakdown, failed relationships, childhood trauma, abusive words, failure, cruelty, anger, resentment, and hurt, while God desires you to have forgiveness-led freedom from resentment, anger, anxiety, defeat, fear, and heartache.

Aside from the spiritual warfare unforgiveness can wreak on you, there are also proven physical and psychological effects that happen when we live with bitterness and resentment (Johns Hopkins Medicine 2024). All things considered, is it hard to imagine why God would command us to forgive?

So often we become bitter without even being honest with ourselves about it. We may lie and say things like:

*It's not a big deal.*

*I'm over it.*

*What's done is done.*

*I'm just going to move on.*

Or we may develop unhealthy coping mechanisms that aren't actually allowing us to cope at all:

- *Binging unhealthy food*
- *Doom scrolling*
- *Withdrawing from our friends and family*
- *Avoiding what we typically enjoy*
- *Avoiding talking about the hurt we've experienced*
- *Numbing ourselves through denial or even substances*

Did either of the above two lists resonate with you? Which ones and why? And, more importantly, what do you intend to do about it?

_____
_____
_____
_____
_____
_____
_____
_____

God wants us to forgive others not for their benefit, but for our own. We cannot live in peace when we have a spirit that is broken and hurting. We certainly cannot move on from that hurt without leaning into God's grace and forgiveness to extend it forward, taking our power back from the person who hurt us, forgiving whatever pain they have caused us, and breaking the bondage that ties us to them. Forgiveness does not mean that we have to agree with or accept what the other person has done, or even like that person. It does mean that we can separate ourselves from them, forgive the feelings they have caused, and focus on our own healing.

## JOURNAL

Today's topic was heavy. Forgiving can still be so difficult to do, even when we have a better understanding of what it is. I want you to reflect on the emotions and feelings that you wrote down earlier. How are they holding you back from healing and stepping into peace? I would challenge you to write a letter to whoever hurt you and offer your forgiveness—don't worry, you don't have to send it. This is not for them but for you. If you find this to be too difficult, or you're just not there yet, I would challenge you to pray to God for guidance and also write about why. There are so many amazing resources out there related to forgiveness— books, podcasts, therapists, and TED Talks. If you have something extra heavy that you just can't work through in these short few pages, I would urge you to look into those resources. It is a crucial step to gaining peace.

_____
_____
_____
_____
_____
_____
_____
_____
_____
_____
_____
_____
_____
_____
_____
_____
_____
_____

## PRAYER

*Heavenly Father,*

*I come before You today with a heart that longs for Your peace and healing. I know that You have called me to forgive, just as You have forgiven me. Lord, I confess that there are people in my life whom I have struggled to forgive, and I recognize that withholding forgiveness has bound me in chains. Today, I ask for Your strength and grace to break those chains and release any bitterness, anger, or hurt that I am holding onto. Teach me to forgive as You have forgiven me, knowing that forgiveness doesn't always mean reconciliation, but trusting You with the hurt and pain. I surrender my desire for revenge, justice, and control into Your hands. I choose to forgive, not because the other person wants or deserves it, but because You have shown me grace and mercy.*

*Lord, I pray that by forgiving others, You will set me free from the burden of resentment and that I will experience the freedom and peace that comes from walking in Your forgiveness. Break every chain of unforgiveness, bitterness, and anger, and fill my heart with Your love and peace.*

*In Jesus' name, I pray.*

*Amen.*

Step 5

# Peace

# Day Nine

## Seeking Spiritual Peace

♫ Playlist: Same God

"Because of the LORD's great love we are not consumed, for his compassions never fail. They are new every morning; great is your faithfulness. I say to myself, 'The LORD is my portion; therefore I will wait for him.' The LORD is good to those whose hope is in him, to the one who seeks him; it is good to wait quietly for the salvation of the LORD. It is good for a man to bear the yoke while he is young. Let him sit alone in silence, for the LORD has laid it on him. Let him bury his face in the dust— perhaps there is hope. Let him offer his cheek to the one who would strike him, and let him be filled with disgrace. For no one is cast off by the Lord forever. Though he brings grief, he will show compassion, so great is his unfailing love. For he does not willingly bring affliction or grief to anyone" (Lamentations 3:22-33).

*Because of the Lord's great love, we are not consumed.* As we near the end of our journey together, I hope there is one great takeaway you find. If nothing else has resonated with you in these last few days, I pray this will— Peace, real peace, the peace we all so desperately desire, is not the absence of difficulty, but the presence of God, Christ, and the Holy Spirit in your life. Peace is the strength, wisdom, and faith to get through those hard things by resting on God's promises. In today's scripture, we are again reassured that even though we face difficulties, heartache, and crises, there is always hope. Every single day God's grace and mercy are renewed and we can find rest in Him. In our waiting, God is always actively moving and preparing us for His greater plans. And I know the waiting is not fun. In fact, I know that waiting can cause us to feel hurt, anger, or even abandonment. But faith comes in when we believe that no matter what our feelings are right now in this moment, we will be able to look back and know exactly why it happened that way— when you have a testimony to share and can be the rock for someone in their own season of waiting; when you realize that the heartbreak that you thought would shatter you only taught you strength and resiliency; when a no turned into I've got something better; or, when that severed relationship led to self-healing. Remember, *Yes, I can and I will get through this with God.*

We have talked a lot in this book about your titles and identity through Christ. But, I'd like to take some time to talk about God's titles and identity. Who He is to us. Who He is for you. God is a sanctuary for a weary spirit. He is the keeper of His children. He is the safe space in all of the hard spaces of the world. Throughout the Bible, we see God referred to in some supremely powerful and beautiful ways.

*El Shaddai - God Almighty*
*El Elyon - The Most High God*
*Jehovah Jireh - The Lord My Provider*
*Jehovah-Raah - The Lord My Shepherd*
*Jehovah Rapha - The Lord Who Heals*

*Jehovah Shalom - The Lord My Peace*
*Jehovah Nissi - The Lord My Banner*

And that is just a small part of the list. As today's worship song reminds us, God was not just these things in the stories of the Bible. God continues to be all of these titles today. We worship and have a relationship with the same God that we read about. God is still almighty and the most high, He is our provider and shepherd, He is a God that heals and He is our peace. He is a waymaker and a miracle worker, our friend and our father. He is our banner of victory. Our spirit can be at peace because of God's love and His sacrifice through Jesus.

You may have heard the quote *"Greater is He who is in you than he who is in the world,"* which comes from the Bible verse 1 John 4:4. This verse assures us that through Jesus' sacrifice, we have the power of the Holy Spirit within us, which is a power greater than any evil, temptation, or devastation of the world. We have the victory of God within us. Which also means that the enemy is under our feet. *"I have given you authority to trample on snakes and scorpions and to overcome all the power of the enemy; nothing will harm you,"* Jesus tells us in Luke 10:19. Girl, how amazing is it that we have spiritual power within us? The ability to demand, command, and rebuke anything that the enemy may throw at us? Our spirit is not weak or easily shaken and our battles are already defeated through God in us.

So many of the battles we face today come in the appearance of being of the world, but often that is a guise for spiritual battles. Sis, it is so important to take care of your spirit so that you are prepared to fight spiritual battles. The only chance you stand to be victorious over these battles is by submitting yourself and your burdens to God and rejecting the devil and his schemes. Do these things, and the enemy will flee from you (James 4:7). Our spiritual battles require spiritual weapons (2 Corinthians 10:3-5). But what are these spiritual weapons, exactly?

The book of Ephesians describes the armor of God that all Christians must equip themselves with—the belt of truth, the breastplate of righteousness, the shoes of the gospel of peace, the shield of faith, the helmet of salvation, and the sword of the spirit. Unfortunately, we cannot just go out and purchase the armor of God on our next shopping spree. Instead, we gather these spiritual weapons through prayer, reading God's Word, keeping our faith in God, and resting on the authority and power in the name of Jesus. We can only gain spiritual peace by actively taking care of and protecting our spirit. As we discussed on Day One, we cannot do it alone. Our peace does not come from ourselves or our own false sense of control. We are emotional, irrational, imperfect human beings. But we serve an unwavering, all-knowing, perfect God who is for us and works through us if only we leave room for Him.

If we want true spiritual peace, we must:

*Pursue and openly receive Peace with God*
Romans 5:1 "Therefore, since we have been justified through faith, we have peace with God through our Lord Jesus Christ."

*Pursue and openly receive Peace from God*
Philippians 4:7: "And the peace of God, which transcends all understanding, will guard your hearts and your minds in Christ Jesus."

*Pursue and openly receive Peace in Christ*
John 14:27: "Peace I leave with you; my peace I give you. I do not give to you as the world gives. Do not let your hearts be troubled and do not be afraid."

*Pursue and openly receive rest for our soul*
Matthew 11:28: "Come to me, all you who are weary and burdened, and I

will give you rest."

If we want true spiritual peace, we must accept Jesus and be filled with the Holy Spirit. God wants to fill every part of us, each nook, cranny, and hidden place. He wants to fill and permeate every part of your soul. God wants to take what is empty and fill it up. If you are anything like me or the story I shared, you probably have plenty of these nooks and crannies within you just waiting to be filled with the Holy Spirit.

We see an example of this in the story of Jesus and the fisherman in Luke chapter 5. Jesus steps into Simon's empty fishing boat and commands him to drop his nets. Even though Simon insists there is nothing to be caught, he drops his net as Jesus commands, and it is filled with so many fish that his net begins to break. In this story, Jesus sees a need to be met—an empty or lacking place—in this case, the boat. But not only does He notice it, He uses what is empty and then restores and fills it—above and beyond what would be expected. Jesus is able even when we've been unable. He is capable of restoring all of our lost and empty spaces if we just put our trust in Him. God is always talking to you, always guiding you, through the power of the Holy Spirit. Are you postured in a way to not only hear Him but listen?

God holds all of His names and titles because He is a God who protects, provides, heals, and leads His children. We can only have true peace through Him, the provider of all our needs. Today's scripture reminds us that the Lord is our portion. This means that He is the ultimate source of all that we need. He provides for us, sustains us, and He is sufficient. There is nothing else we need.

## JOURNAL

Today, I would encourage you to read Ephesians chapter 6 and better acquaint yourself with the armor of God. Which pieces of armor are you lacking? What steps could you take to build up these lacking areas, so you can better equip yourself to protect against spiritual attack and maintain your peace?

_____
_____
_____
_____
_____
_____
_____
_____
_____
_____
_____

## PRAYER

*Lord God, thank you for being my provider, protector, and healer. In the midst of my struggles and hurts, provide me with strength, wisdom, and faith. Remind me to rest in you when I just can't do it alone. God, I know that in my waiting you are always working all things out for my good and the purpose of your will. I pray that I am malleable during these times— ready to hear your voice and answer your call. Ready to step out in whatever direction I am called. God, thank you for being my peace. I know that true peace comes only through surrendering to you and trusting you in all things. When I am weak or shaken, remind me of all the titles you hold and the power you wield. Help me to recognize where I have weakness in my armor and give me guidance on how to strengthen it. Lord, I promise to pursue and openly receive you each and every day. Thank you for your love and provision.*

*In Jesus' name, I pray,*
*Amen.*

# Day Ten

## Peace I Leave With You

🎵 Playlist: The Blessing (Live)

*"Peace I leave with you; my peace I give you. I do not give to you as the world gives. Do not let your hearts be troubled and do not be afraid" (John 14:27, NIV).*

Hi, friend. You made it. We are on Day Ten of this journey together! How do you feel? I remember when I was at the beginning of my healing journey, desperately desiring peace, and finding it to be so elusive. So much of the advice I was given at that time was to give it to God. I heard it from my mom and grandpa; I heard it from my best friend. The hard and frustrating part for me was that despite my relationship with Christ, I just didn't know what giving it to God really meant. It felt frustrating. It felt well-meaning but entirely unhelpful. It sounded like pretty words that were essentially a euphemism. Words that didn't validate the weight of what I was going through. But you know when that changed? When I stood at that altar with a stranger, visibly shaking in fear, but made a choice to move forward in faith anyway. I may not have known how, but I was determined to find out, and I was confident God would show me.

I pray that this book has given you some clarity for how you too might step out of fear, into faith, and give it to God. If today you feel clear-headed and focused with a strong sense of direction, that's amazing! If you feel at peace and ready to maintain that peace with everything you have learned in our time together, that is even better. (Get it, girl!) If these past nine days have drudged up a lot of unresolve for you, that is a good starting point too. Pray, spend time with God and in His Word, continue posturing your heart towards Him, and He will give you exactly what you need to continue working through the dust until it settles.

In today's scripture Jesus promises us a sense of peace that the world cannot offer. A peace within your soul and spirit that makes absolutely no sense to those who do not know Jesus. In this passage Jesus also commands us: *do not be troubled or afraid*. And, while that is our ultimate goal, I also want to validate that we are human beings with human emotions. It is what separates us from other creatures in this world! God gave us complex emotions, and there is no guilt or shame in feeling anxious, depressed, stressed, confused, or worried. There is no shame in some days just feeling too heavy.

Each night I lay in bed, below the large sign centered above it that reads *Give it to God and go to sleep*. Every night this is a reminder for me. But you know what? Some nights, I still toss and turn, unable to sleep, filled with anxiety for the next day. But, I remind myself that this is not God's desire for me. I remember that along with emotions and feelings, God also gave us his divine Word through the Bible, He gave us Jesus Christ as a sacrifice, and He gave us the Holy Spirit to live within us. He gave us the ability to reason and learn and grow. Feeling our emotions is okay. Resting in those emotions and becoming bound to them is not okay. God has laid it out for us. He offers the most complete sense of peace available to mankind.

James 2:20 reminds us that *faith without deeds is useless*, and Proverbs 13:4 tells us that *the desires of the diligent are fully satisfied*. Meaning, you must not just have faith that God will heal and restore, but you must also take action by stepping into that faith. I stepped into faith as I walked away from that altar—still scared and anxious—but refusing to be held in the bondage of that any longer. In bed on those restless nights, I take action by praying, rebuking the lies going through my mind, and reminding myself that God has not failed me yet, and He won't start now.

Through surrendering, practicing mindful and intentional gratitude, extending grace and forgiveness to yourselves and others, and accepting Christ's peace, you will continue to build and protect your peace. Focus on what you can control and give the rest to God. Remember your God-given titles and identity when your self-criticism leads you to lies. Consistently challenge your fears by moving faithfully towards God's favor and calling upon your life. Maintain a grateful heart, mind, and spirit that tills your soil, making it rich and prepared to harvest a good seed and crop. And remember—the Peace of God transcends all of our understanding. We can be at peace not because of who we are, but because of who He is. We have peace because Jesus came back and destroyed fear of death and the grave. He came to give us life abundantly. Take your peace and radiate it to others, so that you may be a light in the dark world of someone who needs it. If we can find peace and live in our peace, God's hand can be fully at work in our lives. He will always do what we cannot. He will always restore and redeem us.

God has an anointing upon your life. You are not an accident or a mistake. He knows every hair on your head (Matthew 10:30). He has good plans for you (Jeremiah 29:11). God is within you, so how can you fail (1 John 4:4)? Rest assured, the devil is under your feet (Romans 16:20). He holds no power over you. Do not believe his lies. Focus on God's truth.

I pray that you have found the peace that Jesus has to offer and can rest in Him in order to protect and retain it. I pray that you've gained the discernment to actively revisit what you've learned here when you are in a season that does not feel quite so peaceful. Yes, the world can be hard and scary, but God is bigger than everything you have already faced and everything you will face in the future. Stay near to Him. And remember, on days where you might be feeling weak, worn down, or less-than, there is a Bible verse that can uplift you and remind you to fear not—one for every single day of the year. Girl, God is so good. And so are you. ♥

*The Lord bless you and keep you*

*Make His face shine upon you and be gracious to you*

*The Lord turn His face toward you*

*And give you peace.*

- The Blessing (Kari Jobe, Elevation Worship, and Cody Carnes)

## JOURNAL

Today's exercise is less structured. I want to spend most of our time today reflecting and praying. Look through your entries throughout the last ten days. What are some of your biggest takeaways? What did you learn that you did not know? What were you reminded of? Where have you experienced the most growth? What do you need to continue working on moving forward?

_____
_____
_____
_____
_____
_____
_____
_____
_____
_____
_____
_____

_____
_____
_____
_____
_____
_____
_____
_____
_____
_____
_____

## PRAYER

*Heavenly Father,*

*You are so good. I pray You remind me of that when I lose sight or forget to remind myself. Please continue to guide me on this journey towards peace. Lord, I know not every day will be easy, but I know Your yoke is light and I pray You continue to be with me during the hard times. I pray You guide me in continuing to grow and protect my peace. Thank You for Your sacrifice through Christ Jesus which allows me peace that could never be found in the world. Thank You for loving me enough. Remind me to always look at myself through your eyes. Lead my heart away from self-criticism and comparison, and toward an endless sense of gratitude for what You have provided. Do not allow me to be deceived by the enemy, but grant me discernment that I may always hear your voice and recognize Your will. Protect my mind, heart, and spirit so that I can continue to sow good seeds into my life.*

*In Jesus' name, I pray,*
*Amen.*

# Acknowledgements

First and foremost, I need to thank God for putting this project on my heart. If I can positively impact just one person through these words, it was all well worth it. He gave me a call and vision for what this book turned out to be, and I know it will be exactly what someone needs.

Secondly, my amazing husband. Thank you for taking on the extra laundry, dishes, and running while I sat at the computer for hours on end, often forgetting to eat. Thank you for keeping the snacks coming and reminding me to take a break when I needed it! Thank you for believing in me and never once doubting me when I say I am going to do something. You are always my biggest supporter and the champion of every single one of my dreams. You are the most amazing father and partner, and I am still in awe that God gave me you.

Thank you to my four amazing boys, who have so selflessly allowed me to work well past normal hours. I'm sure it had nothing to do with the fact that I allowed you some extra tv time to keep you occupied! You are my life's purpose. Nothing makes me more proud than being your mom. Roman, you are always a proponent for what is good and true, and I admire that so much about you! Caius, you truly have the most contagious smile in the world and my heart is filled every day by all the love you have to give! Gatlin, you are so blessed with creativity, curiosity, and sensitivity, and I love watching your little mind go to work! Ozzy, you have kept us on our toes from the second we found out you were going to join our world; you keep our house and hearts so full with your wild spirit! You boys are my greatest blessing.

Thank you to my parents for their unconditional love and teaching me from the very beginning the importance of keeping a relationship with God. Thank you to my mom. You have always been my biggest cheerleader and have instilled in me not only a motivation to work hard and do well, but the courage and confidence to believe I can accomplish anything I want to.

Thank you to my Grandma Stein for instilling a love of stories and books. Bedtime stories with you are some of my earliest memories. Thank you to my Grandma and Grandpa Schaefer for being such a profound example of God's love shining through others. You make every single person in our family feel like they must be the most loved. (Don't worry– your secret is safe with me. I won't tell the others that I'm the true favorite!)

Thank you to my biggest support team. My friends that have shown such sincere love and support in everything I've done in life, but especially in this endeavor. You've read the manuscript more times than you would have liked, you've shared and liked and followed all of the posts. You've texted and called with so many encouraging words and outpouring of your love. I am humbled over and over again by the love I have received as I've worked through this process. If ever there was a time I doubted I could do it, it was short lived due to my girls so loudly believing in me.

Thank you to my amazing editor, Brooke Henson, who worked diligently to help perfect this project! Your hours of detailed and meticulous input made the final product what it is.

Thank you to my readers, friends, and family members that have taken the time to read this book. Thank you for supporting my dreams, showing interest in my thoughts, and mostly, thank you for investing in yourself. God loves you. Jesus is real. Love, and Good, and Light, are the strongest spiritual forces in the world and can overcome any darkness. Don't let the world or the enemy ever fool you into thinking otherwise. I love you all. ♥

## About the Author:

Britton George is a mother, wife, educator, and life-long learner. She lives in Idaho with her husband, four children, and a variety of animals that add joy and adventure (a nice way of saying chaos) to their home. As a school psychologist, she is passionate about supporting and promoting mental well being and advocating for the needs of individuals, while also celebrating their strengths. When she's not writing or reading, Britton enjoys treasure hunting at her local thrift store, camping, and spending quality time with her family. She loves traveling whenever possible, exploring new places, and creating memories with her loved ones. Her experiences as a mother, wife, professional, and Christian woman deeply influence her writing—which was a direct calling on her life by God. While Ten Days to Peace is her debut book, she has already began work on her second and has plans for a third.

Britton Mikael George
writtenby_britton

**Sources**

"Forgiveness: Your Health Depends on It." Johns Hopkins Medicine, January 21, 2024.
> https://www.hopkinsmedicine.org/health/wellness-and-prevention/forgiveness-your-health-depends-on-it

Rauch, Allison. "Butterfly Effect | Chaos Theory, Popular Culture, & Facts." Encyclopedia Britannica, December 21, 2024. https://www.britannica.com/science/butterfly-effect.

"Mental Illness." National Institute of Mental Health. Accessed January 29, 2025. https://www.nimh.nih.gov/health/statistics/mental-illness.

www.ingramcontent.com/pod-product-compliance
Lightning Source LLC
Chambersburg PA
CBHW071232090426
42736CB00014B/3054